Survive and Thrive

Advance Praise

"As John says, there is no shortage of opportunity today, but there is a shortage of execution. If you can focus on creating real solutions to real problems for real people, you'll have a clear advantage in the marketplace. *Survive and Thrive* can show you how."

— **Michael Hyatt**, Entrepreneur, *New York Times* Best-Selling Author of *Platform*

"*Survive and Thrive* provides timeless information about starting a business from scratch, but at exactly the right time. Having gone through a layoff myself in 2008, I know exactly how important each and every lesson John shares is, and I wish this book was around when I first started my entrepreneurial journey. Step by step, genuine, and highly recommended."

— **Pat Flynn**, Entrepreneur *Wall Street Journal* Best-Selling Author of *Will it Fly?*

"The world has changed yet again, and as an entrepreneur, you must rise to the occasion. John's book gives you a step-by-step plan to serve the new market in a new way. Your business is about to be stronger than ever."

— **Mike Michalowicz**, Entrepreneur *Wall Street Journal* Best-Selling Author of *Fix This Next*

"This book provides a step-by-step plan to help you reach more people, make sales, and enjoy more profit, regardless of what the 'economy' is doing. Does it feel like times are tough? *Survive and Thrive* slices through the clutter and helps entrepreneurs build stronger-than-ever businesses while making the world a better place."

— **Ray Edwards**, Entrepreneur Amazon Best-Selling Author of *How to Write Copy That Sells*

"Too many entrepreneurs rely on a booming economy or favorable external circumstances for their business success, but everyone knows this doesn't last forever. If you'd like to build a business that can survive and even thrive when the going gets tough (and it will), then you need this book."

— **Allan Dib**, Entrepreneur
Amazon Best-Selling Author of *The 1-Page Marketing Plan*

"When times are challenging, it is easy for the would-be entrepreneur to slide down into dejection, certain that all effort is futile. John Meese's new book *Survive and Thrive* is the antidote to passive languor. It is a surefire call-to-action that omits all those cliched motivational slogans and guides the reader into the specific activities that will build a business. Not only will it put a bounce in your step and set your chin to a jaunty new jut, *Survive and Thrive* will tell you just what to do today to reach your destination tomorrow."

— **Rabbi Daniel Lapin**, Entrepreneur
Amazon Best-Selling Author of *Thou Shall Prosper*

"Are you struggling to adapt your old business to the new market and grow despite an uncertain economy? Buy this book, put these principles to work, and you're already on the right track."

— **Phillip Stutts**, Entrepreneur, Author of *Fire Them Now*

"*Survive and Thrive* is a recipe for success for any entrepreneur. John has applied these foundational principles in his own businesses and knows first-hand how to ensure your vision and passion become a reality. Every business owner and operator needs this as a handbook now more than ever."

— **Casey Graham**, Entrepreneur, CEO of Gravy Solutions

Survive and Thrive

How to Build a Profitable Business in Any Economy (Including This One)

JOHN MEESE

NEW YORK

LONDON • NASHVILLE • MELBOURNE • VANCOUVER

Survive and Thrive

How to Build a Profitable Business in Any Economy (Including This One)

Published in New York, New York, by Morgan James Publishing. Morgan James is a trademark of Morgan James, LLC. www.MorganJamesPublishing.com

All Scripture quotations, unless otherwise indicated, are taken from The Holy Bible, New International Version®, NIV®.

Morgan James BOGO™

A **FREE** ebook edition is available for you or a friend with the purchase of this print book.

CLEARLY SIGN YOUR NAME ABOVE

Instructions to claim your free ebook edition:
1. Visit MorganJamesBOGO.com
2. Sign your name CLEARLY in the space above
3. Complete the form and submit a photo of this entire page
4. You or your friend can download the ebook to your preferred device

ISBN 9781631953361 paperback
ISBN 9781631953378 ebook
Library of Congress Control Number: 2020946793

Cover and Interior Design by:
Chris Treccani
www.3dogcreative.net

Illustrations by:
Emily Mills of Flavor Graphics

Author Photo by:
Kristin Sweeting Photography

Morgan James is a proud partner of Habitat for Humanity Peninsula and Greater Williamsburg. Partners in building since 2006.

Get involved today! Visit
MorganJamesPublishing.com/giving-back

For my dad, and every other hard-working entrepreneur
who built the world we have the privilege to live in today.

Table of Contents

Introduction: The Great Reset   xiii

Chapter 1:   The Entrepreneur's Paradox   1
Chapter 2:   Pick Your People   17
Chapter 3:   Sell Your Solution   35
Chapter 4:   Court Your Customer   49
Chapter 5:   Choose Your Path   65
Chapter 6:   The Selling Story   77
Chapter 7:   Above and Beyond   91
Chapter 8:   Predict, Don't Prophesy   105
Chapter 9:   Prioritize Profit First   121
Chapter 10:   Charge Up Front   135

Conclusion   151
Acknowledgments   158
Thank You   160
About the Author   161
Additional Resources   163
Endnotes   165

Introduction:

The Great Reset

D o you remember where you were at the beginning of 2020, when terms like "social distancing" and "quarantine" became commonplace as "pandemic" was tossed around in conversation?

What about the first time you heard the words "coronavirus" or "COVID-19"?

On March 11, 2020, the World Health Organization officially declared that the Novel Coronavirus Disease, COVID-19, had become a global pandemic.[1] The disease had been spreading for months, but that moment is when the world took notice and rushed to respond.

World leaders ordered unprecedented lockdowns in an effort to stop the spread of the disease, in many places closing "non-essential businesses" or simply forcing people to stay inside.[2]

What began as a health crisis quickly became an economic crisis all across the globe.

It's hard to capture the full extent of the economic destruction that followed; it may be decades before we fully understand it. Globally, hundreds of millions of people were forced into extreme poverty immediately, and even rich countries like the U.S. were suddenly left with more than 20 million people unemployed.[3]

Just one month into the pandemic, the International Monetary Fund classified the economic crisis as the "worst economic downturn since the Great Depression" and gave it a name: the Great Lockdown.[4]

To try to get a grip on the situation for small business owners, the U.S. Census Bureau started running a "Small Business Pulse Survey"[5] every week. The results were not promising. Immediately, 90% of business owners reported a moderate or large negative impact to their business with 74% reporting declining revenue.

Just a month and a half into the crisis, 35% of business owners reported they had missed a recent payment on a bill or loan. By the end of June, 32% of small business owners reported they had less than one month of cash available to continue operations (another 11% simply said they didn't know how long their cash would keep them afloat).[6]

Suffice it to say the economic damage is devastating. Many businesses are permanently closed because they could not absorb the economic impact, and many others will take years to recover.[7] Like anything else in life, it takes much longer to build something than to destroy it.

There Is No V-Shaped Recovery

Despite the initial claim of many politicians hoping to comfort their constituents, there will be no "V-shaped recovery" from this economic crisis. There is no "snap back" to the economy before the Great Lockdown unless you mean a snap similar to the one Tony Stark gave his life for on the big screen in 2019.

Yes, I am referring to a movie based on a comic book, but if you've been following the box office blockbusters in the Marvel Cinematic University, the idea of "snapping back" might sound very familiar.

Indeed, in *Avengers: Endgame*,[8] the entire movie revolves around a broken band of superheroes fighting to collect enough powerful gems known as "infinity stones" to pull off a single snap that could undo the damage the bad guy, Thanos, had caused in the previous movie *Avengers: Infinity War*[9] when he wiped out exactly half of the population of the universe.

Spoiler alert: The Avengers win! They succeeded in collecting all of the infinity stones and completing a "snap back" to restore the missing half of the universe population, including 50% of humanity. Success! Only... this is where the story becomes eerily relevant to those of us living through the recovery from the Great Lockdown and COVID-19.

As people come back to their homes, their businesses, and start to rebuild their lives, the world is filled with scars of the recent past. Even with a successful snap back in *Avengers: Endgame*, half of humanity had been missing for five years! *Spider-Man: Far From Home*[10] explores how the "new normal" looks less like restoration and more like the beginning of a new, broken world.

That's the type of snap back we should expect as the world recovers from the COVID-19 crisis and parts of the world reopen after extended lockdowns. I say that not to discourage you, but to ask you to accept this reality and embrace it. Only once we acknowledge the reality of the recovery trajectory can we embrace a strategy to rebuild.

We Never Went Back to Life Before 9/11

For most of us living through COVID-19, we can still remember September 11, 2001, in vivid detail. On that day, our world changed forever.

The most immediate change was felt by 2,996 people who died in the terrorist attacks in the World Trade Center, the Pentagon, and the four airplanes, along with the 6,000 others who were injured and the friends and family they all left behind. But the damage didn't stop there.[11]

Over the next decade of war, more than half a million people died violent deaths in the middle east, and back at home, there are scars all over the United States.[12]

After the initial fear of airplane travel wore off, the newly formed Travel Security Administration became an established agency in every airport in the country. The USA Patriot Act, which is still active in 2020, gave the U.S. government unprecedented freedom to spy on every American citizen without a warrant.[13]

My point is: That was one moment in history more than a decade ago, and we still have not "snapped back." As I'm writing this, the current crisis has already lasted for months and the devastation has only begun.

If this is the first time you've read anything I've written, you might think I'm all doom and gloom—but I'm not! I simply want to acknowledge the gravity of the current crisis and make sure you and I are on the same page so we can focus on a step-by-step plan for how we respond.

Jeff Bezos, founder and CEO of Amazon, is well known for his business philosophy that every day is "Day 1" and we get to make decisions to design the future based on a fresh, new perspective each day.[14]

Right now, that philosophy is more important now than ever, because today (and tomorrow) is Day 1 for the global economy. More personally, today is Day 1 for you and me in our business endeavors.

Turn It Off, and Turn It Back On Again

There is a common joke in the tech community that if anyone complains something isn't working, the solution is to turn it off and turn it back on again.

For whatever reason, this works with computers (I'm sure there is a technical explanation). If your phone or computer isn't working as expected, go ahead and call the tech support line and you'll see what I mean. The first thing they'll ask you to do is to turn it off and turn it back on again.

When I started studying economics, I quickly realized there were serious problems with the shaky foundation of the twenty-first century global economy. When I worked at a business and economics research lab, I joked with my nerdy economist friends that we should just "turn it off and turn it back on again" to fix the economy—but I was kidding! I never thought that was actually a good idea.

Nevertheless, here we are. For all intents and purposes, the Great Lockdown shut down the global economy. Many businesses were able to still function in some capacity during that lockdown, and many others found a way to adapt, but countless restaurants, boutiques, and other brick-and-mortar businesses were forced to close their doors for weeks or months.

It will take years for us to calculate the extent of the financial damage this created, but it is safe to say that this was catastrophic to the small business community. Someone hit the reset button on the economy. In fact, the World Economic Forum has officially dubbed this era the "Great Reset." It's not all doom and gloom, either:

> "From a technology standpoint, the future that everyone talked about before the pandemic is now here, ahead of schedule. We expected significant advancements in digitizing our world, in adopting new business models, and in generating outcomes for students, patients, researchers, and community members like never before. Today, that is no longer a prediction; it is reality. The COVID-19 crisis was the catalyst for rapid change, and it presents the opportunity for us to collectively shift priorities, refocus on what matters, and accelerate to a brighter future."[15]

The first businesses to close permanently were those who relied on a daily influx of cash and already had a pile of debt accumulating behind their operations. As I write this, many small businesses are still struggling along from day to day, waiting for recovery, and don't realize they are today's walking dead.

 The Great Lockdown was a death sentence to many businesses, but out of that death comes new life and opportunity in the Great Reset.

To be clear, I have no desire to minimize the health ramifications of the COVID-19 pandemic. Many people died, and many more people became consumed by the fear of death that made it impossible for them to live their otherwise normal daily lives.

That said, the economic impact is no laughing matter. Across the world, the small business community is the source of many people's employment (in the U.S., nearly half of all jobs come from small businesses).[16] A death sentence for small business is a poverty sentence to many families who had no way to foresee this financial storm.

Where Do We Go from Here?

There is a lot of hope tied to the power of the U.S. government (and other world powers) to pour seemingly endless amounts of money into the pockets of business owners and employees to keep them afloat.

From the get-go, it was clear that this was a pipe dream, despite the best of intentions and unprecedented support of the small business community from world governments like the United States (who provided more than $1 trillion in business relief funding).[17]

Like using a garden hose to replace a waterfall, the government programs were doomed from the start. It is up to us, the entrepreneurs, to solve the problems (that we didn't create).

The world needs you and your business to thrive, to lift us up on your shoulders and start refilling the world with wealth. Wealth, after all, is a reward for serving each other, for creating real solutions to real problems for real people, all over the world.

There is an entire army of medical professionals working on the solution to the health crisis, and I commend them for it and pray for their success. What we need now is an entire army of entrepreneurs working on the economic crisis, so we can rebuild our world stronger, wealthier, and more resilient than ever before.

There is no shortage of opportunity today, but there is a shortage of execution. Will you roll up your sleeves and help build the new world, starting with your own business? Are you with me?

Entrepreneurs, assemble!

How to Get the Most Out of Reading This Book

You're a busy entrepreneur, and you don't need another stack of pages on your shelf—you need a tactical battle plan to build (or rebuild) your business so you can survive and thrive in any economy. Yes, that includes the current economy, pandemic and all!

In this book, I lay out a roadmap to building an unshakeable core to your business based on timeless business principles that are always important but are especially important right now. Building a core foundation of finance, marketing, and sales strategies that have stood the test of time will allow you to adapt your current business, or build a new business, in any economy.

I've created a free online assessment you can use to assess your business right now to get your business ThriveScore, which evaluates your business based on the core fundamentals and gives you a numerical score. Each chapter in this book will help you shore up your business in one of nine key areas, all of which are reflected in your business ThriveScore.

Right now, go ahead and get your initial ThriveScore so you can get a complimentary business assessment to know where you're starting from, by visiting YourThriveScore.com.

I recommend reading this book through once, cover to cover, and highlighting or earmarking concepts you want to revisit. That gives you a comprehensive overview of the framework presented. Then revisit each chapter, sequentially, and implement the strategy in question. Periodically, revisit YourThriveScore.com to watch your score (and your bank account) grow.

The business fundamentals within this book aren't original, but they are practical. I've adopted these principles in my own business ventures after learning from a healthy mix of trial and error, breakthrough business books, and interviews with dozens of today's entrepreneurs. I've published most of these interviews on my podcast, which you can listen to yourself at SurviveAndThriveInterviews.com.

This book is yours; please make the most of it—and keep up the good work!

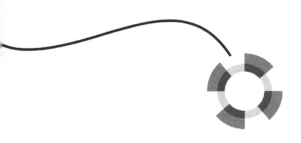

Chapter 1:

The Entrepreneur's Paradox

Real Entrepreneurs Get Paid—But They Don't Work for Money

What does it mean to be an entrepreneur?

Sure, we'll get into the specifics of how to succeed as an entrepreneur and the mechanics of building a profitable business throughout this book, but, first things first, we need to set the stage.

Entrepreneur comes from the French word "entreprendre" for "undertake" (which I suppose makes me an undertaker). Merriam-Webster defines an entrepreneur[18] as "one who organizes, manages, and assumes the risks of a business or enterprise." While that definition may be correct, it's painfully vague. That definition isn't really helpful day to day as an entrepreneur.

Merriam-Webster's definition may sound official, but there are many competing definitions of what it means to be an entrepreneur. As one group of economists put it in a 2008 attempt to define the term, "Although entrepreneurship has become a buzzword in the public debate, a coherent definition of entrepreneurship has not yet emerged."[19]

Better yet, the Federal Reserve Bank of Minneapolis published an article leading with "Wanted: Entrepreneurs (Just don't ask for a job description)."[20]

So, what is an entrepreneur, really? What does it really mean, day to day, to be an entrepreneur?

That's a really important question because if you and I are going to be effective entrepreneurs, then first we have to recognize and understand what it means to be an entrepreneur. Why do we exist?

Many sources define an entrepreneur as someone who is willing to take on risk for the sake of reward, and that is somewhat true because you do need to have a reasonable tolerance for risk to shake off the shackles of employment and set out on your own—but the truth of what it means to be an entrepreneur is much more simple, clear, and important.

 Entrepreneurs are people who solve problems for a profit.

That's the definition Michael Hyatt uses[21], and as a *New York Times* bestselling author who has built an eight-figure company from scratch, serving business leaders and entrepreneurs across the globe (not to mention his previous career as the CEO of Thomas Nelson Publishers), Michael knows what he is talking about.

I think this definition is the most apt because it captures the key important aspects of what it truly means to be an effective entrepreneur. Entrepreneurs are problem solvers.

So yes, an entrepreneur is someone who solves a problem for a profit.

Entrepreneurship has little or nothing to do with whether or not you are self-employed. Entrepreneurship is a mindset and a way of life. If you solve a problem for a profit, you are an entrepreneur. If not, you're welcome to become one.

If you create a product, but it does not solve a problem, you don't have a business. That will become painfully clear as you wait for customers who never appear.

If you have a product or service that can solve a real problem for real people, but you don't make money doing it, you don't have a business. At best, you have a charity or pet project, but you may have a failing business (if that is the case, keep reading and we'll work together to fix your business throughout this book).

Profit is important; it is a clear qualifier of what it means to be an entrepreneur, but does that mean that entrepreneurship is all about making money? Is that the purpose of business at the end of the day?

Some people would say so, but that's never been my approach. Sure, I want to make money from the work I do—and my wife and kids want the same thing as well—but I like to think of profit as a report card for how well I've served humanity.

Entrepreneurship is simultaneously all about money and not really about money at all. That's not a contradiction, it's a paradox. The entrepreneur's paradox. As an entrepreneur, the path to profits is through serving people.

Profit is an unquestionable metric. It takes a complete process of creating a real solution to a real problem for real people to generate profit. Not only that, but to generate profit you have to get people's attention (marketing) and persuade them to purchase your solution (sales) while simultaneously managing the incoming dollars and outgoing dollars to end the day with more than you started with (finance).

Entrepreneurship is exciting, but it's not for the faint of heart. The vast majority of people never become full-time entrepreneurs, but everyone on the planet relies on entrepreneurs for the world we live in. Of course, entrepreneurs didn't create the planet we live on, but entrepreneurs got people to work together and trade eggs for milk, which allowed people to specialize in raising cows or chickens, which in turn allowed everyone to get more efficient and generate wealth.

Over time, that wealth allowed people to build towns and establish general stores where people could trade what they had for what they needed or wanted, and the world continued to grow.

Today, most of us are privileged to live in a world where we can eat food, drink water, and wear clothes without ever having to raise our own food or sew our own clothes because, as a worldwide group of generations of people, we've followed the call of the entrepreneur.

The entrepreneur innovates, solves problems, and sees opportunities where other people see pain. The entrepreneur is the builder, creator, or visionary who sees the future and chases it, inspiring other people to follow along.

Yes, an entrepreneur solves a problem for a profit on the granular, individual level—but when thousands of entrepreneurs solve thousands of problems for billions of dollars in profit, everyone in the present *and future* reaps the benefits with a healthier, wealthier world with less problems (or perhaps new problems, but still the growth is the same).

If you're still reading this, then chances are you, yourself, are an entrepreneur or you are inspired to become an entrepreneur, and both are noble pursuits.

If you are not inspired to solve problems for a profit, then you need to pause first to ask yourself why.

Solving problems is about more than your own problem with your checking account; it's about serving other people by getting to know their needs and creatively serving those needs. Are you willing to set aside your own needs to serve your fellow human?

It's a bit counterintuitive, but if you do that you will be rewarded financially in return. Hence, the entrepreneur's paradox.

Let's Talk about Profit and Wealth

Your business has the potential to generate more wealth than any other opportunity on the planet (other than, perhaps, another business). Unfortunately, your business also has the potential to rack up more expenses than any other opportunity on the planet. Think of this as the First Law of Financial Dynamics (which I made up). It states:

> *Wealth cannot be created from scratch; it can only change form—unless you're an entrepreneur.*

Alright, let's make sure we're on the same page with our terms here. At the end of the day, what is profit, actually? Sure, we all want it (usually we want lots of it)—but why?

Initially, the answer seems obvious. We need money; first to pay the bills and next to buy and do things we and our loved ones enjoy. Money is a means to an end, the fuel for our lifestyle—and profit is the only money in business that you get to keep.

Is that all profit is, then? The leftover money that you get to keep? Not really. For your business, profit is a success score based on how well you've managed to create real solutions to real problems for real people (remember, as a business owner, that is your actual job).

Profit is a result of both efficacy and efficiency.

Your efficacy (or effectiveness) is measured by the revenue you generate, but that's a deceivingly simple answer. How much revenue you generate is determined by how clear your purpose is, who your business is designed to serve, how well your customers perceive you are at fulfilling that purpose, and how many people know you and your business exist.

Efficiency is the simpler (if not easier) metric. Measured by your business expenses, efficiency is the amount of time, energy, and money it takes to fulfill your purpose—at least, as well as you are fulfilling it right now.

Many aspects of business are subjective, or hard to measure, but not profit. Profit is an unquestionable metric. At any given moment, you can accurately measure your profit in your business, if there is any. If there isn't any profit, you have a problem (but we will fix that).

There's a deeper significance of profit than simply the accounting equation, which Rabbi Daniel Lapin gets at in his book *Thou Shalt Prosper*, where he says, "When you serve the marketplace, they will give you certificates of appreciation with Presidents' faces on them."

Rabbi Daniel is a traditional Orthodox Jewish Rabbi, as well as an author, speaker, and a bit of a business analyst. When I interviewed him, he expounded on this idea further to explain how, at the end of the day, financial wealth is actually a reflection of your character.

He pointed out that you can take a sample group of 1,000 people who have an identical financial earning history, with the same age and qualifications, who have had roughly the same kind of jobs for roughly the same amount of time, and yet find vastly different financial outcomes. As he says,

"So, you'd think that if economics was a pure science, which it obviously isn't, we could now predict the net worth of each of those thousand men. Right? Because they've all made exactly the same amount of money. But you see, whether you save and invest or whether you spend and consume is a character issue, not an economic issue. It has to do with your soul. And so, it's shocking to many people. But it shouldn't be a surprise to any thoughtful person. In that thousand cohort of statistics, it ranges from people who have several million dollars of assets and negligible liabilities to people whose net worth is negative."[22]

Does the idea of profit make you uncomfortable? That idea may sound laughable to some, but I live in the South of the United States and this is a prevalent issue. Countless entrepreneurs sabotage their success because they are uncomfortable with the idea of becoming wealthy at the expense of others, and so they lower their prices or hold themselves back.

If that's you, I want to remind you that people need you (the unusual entrepreneur) to generate profit. The more profit you generate, the bigger problems you've solved, and the more resources you have access to in order to solve bigger problems for bigger profits, the better off the world will be for it.

So, yes, serve the market—which really means serve the people, and as public servants pay close attention to your incoming certificates of appreciation to make sure that you are offering real solutions to real problems for real people, consistently over time.

Welcome to the 21st Century Economy

While entrepreneurship is as old as human society itself, today's economy has its own unique characteristics that are worth exploring briefly to set the stage for the business you're building today.

Whether you make things to sell, sell things other people made, or design ideas of things to sell, you are in marketing. We are all in marketing today.

At its core, marketing is getting people's attention, or creating demand. A market is made of both supply and demand, but over the last century, a massive shift took place in the global economy where it now rarely matters who controls supply.

Think about it. You can use 3D printing technology or print-on-demand facilities to make almost anything you can think of and send that directly to customers without ever touching the product yourself. You can upload a book to the internet that you wrote on your laptop and *voila*! You're a self-published author (although I worked with a publisher for the book in your hands).

You can use crowdfunding platforms like Kickstarter or Patreon to get individual people all over the world to fund your next product or business idea. With almost any piece of information only a few clicks away, the supply-focused economy is over.

Welcome to the Attention Economy. That's the term coined by Nobel prize-winning economist Herbert A. Simon in 1997, when he identified that "a wealth of information creates a poverty of attention."[23]

Sure, there are still some business owners clinging to the old world, hoarding their secrets and sending cease and desist letters to anyone who tries to sell something similar, but they are a dying breed. Most business owners have begun to wake up to the fact that today's economy isn't about owning supply, it's about owning demand.

If you have thousands of followers on social media or subscribers to your email list, you have people's attention. Businesses recognize that you have the access they need, so they will gladly pay you for the privilege of access to the people who are paying attention to you.

If you have a one-of-a-kind revolutionary product that you want to sell, once upon a time you could have shopped that around to distributors who may have signed a contract with you to sell the product, exclusively, to people all over the world. Now, you can easily list your product on Amazon, eBay, or your own website to sell your product—but that's useless unless you have people's attention to examine your product and potentially buy.

The Attention Economy is alive and well, but another socioeconomic shift is taking place as I'm writing this book.

As the Age of Information spread massive amounts of data across the world over the last half-century, and technology created a peer-to-peer connection between people all over the planet, excitement turned to overwhelm as people realized that there was simply too much data to process on any topic, at any time.

As functioning humans in the twenty-first century, we've learned to filter out and ignore hundreds of notifications, reminders, ads, and announcements every day.

The promise of unlimited access to anything you want to know about any topic in the world was exciting when the Age of Information began, and the internet sped up the pace of communication, but as venture capitalist Mary Meeker put it, "We are awash in data, but lacking connectivity and insight."[24]

As individuals and organizations drown in data, they increasingly look to topical experts to make some sense of the available information and provide simple-to-understand insight. That's become true at the individual level, where we seek out expert personalities we trust on topics we care about, and it's become true at the organizational level where governments partner with technology startups to understand the landscape of the world they both live and work in.

Because of the nearly unlimited access to information that came with the internet, a generation of armchair philosophers took to social media with self-educated analysis of what to do with the world. Over time, that's become less palatable as more and more people tune out the noise to tune into the specialist, guru, or trusted authority on whatever topic is in question at the time.

Antonio Neri, CEO of Hewlett Packard Enterprise, published his analysis through the World Economic Forum, to claim that "COVID-19 ended the Information Era and ushered in the Age of Insight."[25] As he said,

> "From a technology standpoint, the future that everyone talked about before the pandemic is now here, ahead of schedule. We expected significant advancements in digitizing our world, in adopting new business models, and in generating outcomes for students, patients, researchers, and community members like never before. Today, that is no longer a prediction; it is reality. The COVID-19 crisis was the catalyst for rapid change, and it presents the opportunity for us to collectively shift priorities, refocus on what matters, and accelerate to a brighter future.
>
> "As we recover, it's important to focus on the future. We need to look beyond the goal of becoming digitally powered and instead contemplate how we will be best positioned to deliver outcomes for our stakeholders. The Great Reset challenges us to radically rethink how we make decisions and who benefits from the outcomes—and how to develop and apply technology in new and meaningful ways for the benefit of all."

With the Attention Economy combined with the Age of Insight, there is a massive demand for innovative entrepreneurs to step up to the plate, make sense of the world around us, and communicate a vision for the world ahead.

At the same time, entrepreneurship has been in a dramatic decline for the last several decades, so this transition and the need for entrepreneurs to rise to the challenge is important, more now than ever. As Leigh Buchanan, Editor-at-Large of *Inc.* magazine, highlighted well before the Great Reset,

> "The Kauffman Foundation, citing its own research and drawing on U.S. Census data, concluded that the number of companies less than a year old had declined as a share of all businesses by nearly 44 percent between 1978 and 2012. And those declines swept across industries, including tech. Meanwhile, the Brookings Institution, also using Census data, established that the number of new businesses is down across the country and that more businesses are dying than are being born."[26]

Jim Clifton, CEO of Gallup and author of *Born to Build*, added some fuel to the fire on the importance of this issue, saying,[27]

> "True entrepreneurs are rare—and getting rarer. Yet it is crucial to our economy and national security that we find them... Without a growing entrepreneurial economy, there are no new good jobs... We are focused on innovation. But what we need are entrepreneurs to turn innovations into products, revenue, jobs, and economic growth."

A Word about Problems

The reason why it's important to start this book with this mini-manifesto of sorts is because—whether or not you survive the current crisis or the next crisis and whether or not you thrive—it is entirely dependent upon your mindset and your capability to adapt as an entrepreneur. As Tom Schwab, CEO of Interview

Valet, put it, "One thing about the human condition [is] we're all either in a crisis, coming out of a crisis... or going into a crisis. Right?"[28]

The reality is, yes, problems are hard. Some problems (like a global pandemic and simultaneous economic crisis) are harder than others, but at the end of the day, problems are the reason why we entrepreneurs exist.

The reason why entrepreneurs are on this planet is to solve problems. This is what we're here for. Without problems, the world would not need us. We must be grateful for the problems we have because they are ours to solve. These problems are what gives us meaning and purpose.

Some problems hurt more than others, and some are felt across the world by countless people while other problems are felt by just a few.

 Choosing the path of entrepreneurship means choosing a path of problems for the rest of your professional career.

As uncomfortable as problems are for the best of us, an entrepreneur needs to embrace each problem as an opportunity to create a solution. Without problems, we would not need entrepreneurs!

A massive economic crisis may be a problem too big for you, as one entrepreneur, to resolve, but chances are there are areas where even a global crisis affects your local community or a specific subset of people in a way where you can help them by solving their problems for a profit (yes, you should still make profit during crisis. It's how you get paid).

If thousands of entrepreneurs across the planet simultaneously focus on solving specific, prevalent problems, then that combined effort is what moves humanity forward and creates economic recovery that will last.

Governments and banks will do their best to throw money and policy at problems, and they may mitigate some problems or soften the blow of them, but typically they create new problems by doing so, and the efforts never last.

At best, governments and central banks can prop up an economy long enough to give entrepreneurs time to step in, solve problems, and build something new.

At worst, governments and central banks can gum up the works and make it more difficult for entrepreneurs to step in and innovate, and that happens more often than not.

No matter, the entrepreneur's job is the same: Solve problems for a profit.

Throughout this book, I'll walk you through nine foundational strategies for building a profitable business in any economy, and each of these can and should help you along the way to success, but only if you first remember your job and your important role in the world economy—not just today, but forever!

Think about it. When you solve a real problem today for real people, then those people live a better life and pass that goodness onto their children, whether the change you make be large or small. Generations from now, there will be a new world of technology and lifestyle that we can't even currently imagine, but it will be thanks to the problems you, and a million entrepreneurs like you, solved.

That's the power of entrepreneurship. By itself, your solution may seem small, but with a natural flow of profit as a reward, countless entrepreneurs will create their own solutions and, together, these will exponentially improve the world as if coordinated by an "Invisible Hand."

Because entrepreneurship and business are as old as human society itself, there are certain timeless business principles that apply in any industry any time, and that is the focus of this book.

While technology and marketing strategies change rapidly, the core framework of a thriving business is consistent. The nine foundational strategies throughout this book work together to create a single, thriving organism that is a profitable business. Any one of the nine strategies should improve your business, or business concept, but the strategies are best when implemented all together because they are integrated into a single organism, or machine.

That's, by the way, my definition of a business: An asset that generates wealth. Creating a business requires entrepreneurship (solving problems for a profit), but operating a business over time becomes less focused on innovation and more focused on optimizing efficiency to deliver real solutions to real problems for real people efficiently and effectively. As a living organism, that generates wealth for the owner (along the way providing income to employees and transformation to customers, truly a win-win-win relationship).

Operating a business is its own field of study, and there are phenomenal books available on this topic, such as *Traction*[29] by Gino Wickman or *Clockwork*[30] by Mike Michalowicz. Mike calls this need of a business "Order" and while it is important, Mike and I both agree that marketing, sales, and finance are all far more important because you cannot optimize a business that financially doesn't exist.

This book includes an equal mix of marketing, sales, and finance strategies, which all relate to the flow of money through the living organism of your business, and money is the fuel that feeds your business, your employees, and yourself.

Claim your **FREE business assessment**
($100 value) and unlock additional resources at
YourThriveScore.com

Chapter 2:

Pick Your People

Get Crystal Clarity on Your Target Customer to Serve

Before you get into any marketing mechanics, you need to have clarity on your objective. What are you trying to accomplish? Do you want to gain more clients, get more sales, and generate wealth for your family?

We live in an exciting time. If you know what to do with it, you have access to the attention of anybody, anywhere in the world. So, who are you going to serve? If you had the attention of 1,000 people right now, how would you know if they were the right people to have in the room? What would you share with them, offer to them, and ask them?

Not all customers, or potential customers, are equally valuable to your business. If you're building a business selling dog food and you get 1,000 people to visit your website, walk into your store, or join your email list—but not a single one of them owns a dog—you're stuck.

You need to consider who your business is designed to help, what problems you're prepared to solve, and who actually wants help with their problem(s) at all. Those ingredients should help you start to define your Target Customer.

Countless businesses make the mistake of spending time and money to waste the attention of people who aren't their Target Customer, which does no one any good.

Do you have a clearly defined target customer, including documented details on their behavior and lifestyle? Who are the "real people" your business is serving? That information is what keeps you in business, and it's also what helps you pivot at a moment's notice because you know who you serve.

To illustrate how important this is today, consider the following excerpt from a pivotal article by Kevin Kelly, co-founder of *WIRED*, called "1,000 True Fans."[31]

1,000 True Fans by Kevin Kelly (An Excerpt)

To be a successful creator you don't need millions. You don't need millions of dollars or millions of customers, millions of clients or millions of fans. To make a living as a craftsperson, photographer, musician, designer, author, animator, app maker, entrepreneur, or inventor you need only thousands of true fans.

A true fan is defined as a fan that will buy anything you produce. These diehard fans will drive 200 miles to see you sing; they will buy the hardback and paperback and audible versions of your book; they will purchase your next figurine sight unseen; they will pay for the "best-of" DVD version of your free YouTube channel; they will come to your chef's table once a month. If you have roughly a thousand of true fans like this (also known as super fans), you can make a living—if you are content to make a living but not a fortune.

Here's how the math works. You need to meet two criteria. First, you have to create enough each year that you can earn, on average, $100 profit from each true fan. That is easier to do in some arts and businesses than others, but it is a good creative challenge in every area because it is always easier and better to give your existing customers more, than it is to find new fans.

Second, you must have a direct relationship with your fans. That is, they must pay you directly. You get to keep all of their support, unlike the small percent of their fees you might get from a music label, publisher, studio, retailer, or other intermediate. If you keep the full $100 of each true fan, then you need only 1,000 of them to earn $100,000 per year. That's a living for most folks.

A thousand customers is a whole lot more feasible to aim for than a million fans. Millions of paying fans is not a realistic goal to shoot for, especially when you are starting out. But a thousand fans is doable. You might even be able to remember a thousand names. If you added one new true fan per day, it'd only take a few years to gain a thousand.

***

Fans, customers, patrons have been around forever. What's new here? A couple of things. While direct relationship with customers was the default mode in old times, the benefits of modern retailing meant that most creators in the last century did not have direct contact with consumers. Often even the publishers, studios, labels and manufacturers did not have such crucial information as the name of their customers. For instance, despite being in business for hundreds of years no New York book publisher knew the names of their core and dedicated readers.

For previous creators these intermediates (and there was often more than one) meant you need much larger audiences to have a success. With the advent of ubiquitous peer-to-peer communication and payment systems—also known as the web today—everyone has access to excellent tools that allow anyone to sell directly to anyone else in the world.

So, a creator in Bend, Oregon can sell—and deliver—a song to someone in Katmandu, Nepal as easily as a New York record label (maybe even more easily). This new technology permits creators to maintain relationships, so that the customer can become a fan, and so that the creator keeps the total amount of payment, which reduces the number of fans needed.

This new ability for the creator to retain the full price is revolutionary, but a second technological innovation amplifies that power further. A fundamental virtue of a peer-to-peer network (like the web) is that the most obscure node is only one click away from the most popular node. In other words, the most obscure under-selling book, song, or idea, is only one click away from the best-selling book, song or idea. Early in the rise of the web the large aggregators of content and products, such as eBay, Amazon, Netflix, etc., noticed that the total sales of all the lowest selling obscure items would equal or in some cases exceed the sales of the few best-selling items. Chris Anderson (my successor at Wired) named this effect "The Long Tail," for the visually graphed shape of the sales distribution curve: a low nearly interminable line of items selling only a few copies per year that form a long "tail" for the abrupt vertical beast of a few bestsellers. But the area of the tail was as big as the head. With that insight, the aggregators had great incentive to encourage audiences to click on the obscure items. They invented recommendation engines and other algorithms to channel attention to the rare creations in the long tail. Even web search companies like Google, Bing, Baidu found it in their interests to reward searchers with the obscure because they could sell ads in the long tail as well. The result was that the most obscure became less obscure.

If you lived in any of the 2 million small towns on Earth you might be the only one in your town to crave death metal music, or get turned on by whispering, or want a left-handed fishing reel. Before the web you'd never be able to satisfy that desire. You'd be alone in your fascination. But now satisfaction is only one click away. Whatever your interests as a creator are, your 1,000 true fans are one click from you. As far as I can tell there is nothing—no product, no idea, no desire—without a fan base on the internet. Everything made, or thought of, can interest at least one person in a million—it's a low bar. Yet if even only one out of million people were interested, that's potentially 7,000 people on the planet. That means that any 1-in-a-million appeal can find 1,000 true fans. The trick is to practically find those fans, or more accurately, to have them find you.

Now here's the thing; the big corporations, the intermediates, the commercial producers, are all under-equipped and ill-suited to connect with these thousand true fans. They are institutionally unable to find and deliver niche audiences and consumers. That means the long tail is wide open to you, the creator. You'll have your one-in-a-million true fans to yourself. And the tools for connecting keep getting better, including the recent innovations in social media. It has never been easier to gather 1,000 true fans around a creator, and never easier to keep them near.

***

The takeaway: 1,000 true fans is an alternative path to success other than stardom. Instead of trying to reach the narrow and unlikely peaks of platinum bestseller hits, blockbusters, and celebrity status, you can aim for direct connection with a thousand true fans. On your way, no matter how many fans you actually succeed in gaining, you'll be surrounded not by faddish infatuation, but by genuine and true appreciation. It's a much saner destiny to hope for. And you are much more likely to actually arrive there.

Who Is Your Target Customer?

Kevin Kelly's 1,000 True Fans framework is a great start to thinking through what's possible with a niche-specific target customer, but it doesn't have to stop there. A quick review of *Inc.* magazine's list of the fastest-growing privately held companies in America shows hundreds of multi-million-dollar companies that focused on a specific target customer and created real solutions to real problems for those real people, with massive success.

Companies like ConvertKit, which makes email marketing software for "creators" (think authors, photographers, and YouTubers, for example), or Amherst Madison, a real estate brokerage that hyperfocuses on serving customers in the Boise, Idaho, area with excellence.

Picking a target customer is the most important decision you will make in your business, because everything else you create will stem from that initial decision (similarly, this is a foundational decision for everything else you will learn in this book).

It's no secret that entrepreneurship is a difficult path, with many pitfalls along the way. You're going to take risks; there is no magic solution that's going to remove that risk or guarantee that your business will succeed. When you set out to build a new business, you do so with the knowledge that many who have gone before you have failed.

That said, there is one skill you can cultivate that will significantly increase your chance of success: your empathy advantage.

Cultivate Your Empathy Advantage

It's easy to brush past empathy as another "soft skill" that's nice to have, all things considered. But in the modern world of business, effective empathy is a skill that can make or break your ability to succeed. At its core, empathy is the ability to see life from another person's perspective, to "put yourself in another person's shoes," as the saying goes.

In business, effective empathy allows you to get inside the mind of your target audience and identify problems (from their perspective) that you can help solve. This is the path to creating real solutions to real problems for real people and building a thriving business.

Contrast this with the approach many entrepreneurs take: scratching their own itch by solving their own problems and selling the solution. Sometimes, this works—but only because enough people with the same problem are seeking a solution. Maybe you'll luck out, but it's a risky bet.

Ángel Cabrera, President of George Mason University, put it this way in a report from *Forbes:*[32]

> "At its very heart, a business is the beauty of bringing together people and things to make the community better off—these are the businesses we admire. Empathy is the one tool that makes it all happen."

Empathy is crucial, and it can be an incredible advantage. Regrettably, it's also one of the most overlooked skills, denigrated as an innate skill you either have or you don't.

On the contrary, you can strengthen your empathy advantage like a muscle, starting with the principle "Seek first to understand, then to be understood." This comes directly from Stephen Covey's classic bestseller, *The 7 Habits of Highly Effective People.*

When this approach becomes your priority, every interaction with a potential customer becomes "How can we help you?" instead of "Here's how we can help."

That subtle difference completely shifts the conversation, making your potential customers feel valued. This approach keeps you on track to create products or services that meet the real needs your audience shares.

Effective empathy is a skill that can make or break your ability to succeed.

Your ability to empathize effectively is one of the surest indicators of whether or not you will create a lasting business, regardless of your industry or niche.

Use this to your advantage, and place empathy at the core of your business. With that superpower in place, you'll drastically increase your chance of success. I love how Kevin Whelan, a marketing consultant for coworking spaces, describes his approach to this.[33]

"I think on my tombstone, it's going to say, the answers to your marketing problems are in your customers... I say that over and over again; anyone who asks me a marketing question, I say, who's your target market? And then like, what's their situation? How do you do business with them based on their situation? Not what you think they want, but what are they actually needing."

Michael Hyatt adds this anecdote,[34]

"As an entrepreneur, there's two things you have got to understand to be successful. So, pick your target market. Understand first, what are their aspirations, what do they long for? What do they want? What's the thing they're seeking, above all else, when it comes from a business perspective? And then secondly, what gets in the way? What are the obstacles? What are the challenges, what's keeping them from getting what they want? If you know both of those things, you can create products, you can offer services, it will inform your marketing, copy, everything. And that's really all you have to do to succeed. If you know those two things and go to work solving those problems and helping people get what they want, so that it's faster, easier, and cheaper; you'll be successful."

When you're leveraging your empathy advantage as an entrepreneur, you need to do the personal work of getting to know the real problems your target customer has, in their own words, the way they experience it. Ray Edwards, a master copywriter and author of *How to Write Copy That Sells*, put it this way,[35]

"Now more than ever, you have to be dialed in on who the person is that you're primarily serving, what the problem is you're helping them solve, and what is the pain of that problem in the way that they experience it? Because they may describe it differently than you do.

The example… if you're a weight loss coach, you may be thinking, well, having those extra pounds on you is bad, because it's bad for your cardiovascular systems, could lead to diabetes, could lead to all sorts of arteriosclerosis, all these terrible outcomes for your health—but the way your customer is experiencing that pain is they don't like the way they look when they take off their shirt or when they get in a swimsuit to go to the pool on the beach. So, you've got to talk about the problem and the pain in the way that's relevant to them the way they're experiencing it."

What's the Right Problem to Solve?

Remember, as an entrepreneur, your job is to solve a problem for a profit. First things first, you need to know who you are helping so you can pick a problem to focus on, and the second thing, you need to understand what problems your real people have and which problems you should solve first.

We all think we're different, unique, or special, but in many ways we humans are all the same.

For example, until you have food and water to sustain your body, you don't have the brain power to even think about your outfit for the day, next week's finance meeting, or your 401(k).

Food and water are important for meeting your physiological needs, and they always come first.

Insight like this is important because building an audience is all about building trust. The fastest path to earning people's trust is empathy, which leads people to truly believe you understand them.

If you can clearly articulate how your target customer is already thinking or feeling, they are likely to believe you have the solution to the problem they have, too. So, how do you get inside someone's head to grasp what they need at any given moment? Is there a framework for understanding people through empathy? As a matter of fact, yes.

The empathy advantage is a helpful approach here, but a tool that makes this much easier to quickly jump in and assess current problems is Maslow's Hierarchy of Marketing (my name for Maslow's Theory of Human Motivation, often referred to as Maslow's Hierarchy of Needs).[36]

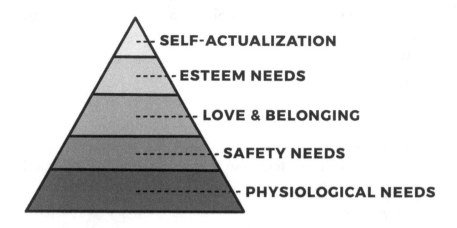

In 1943, Abraham Maslow revolutionized our understanding of human motivation by outlining a hierarchy of needs to explain how people naturally focus on one level of needs at a time. In order:

1. Physiological Needs: Basic bodily needs like food and water
2. Safety Needs: Resources like income and strong health
3. Love and Belonging: Friendship, family, and connection
4. Esteem Needs: Achievement and the respect of others
5. Self-Actualization: Desire to become the best one can be

At any given moment, each person on the planet is focused on one primary category of need, and that is immensely valuable context because you can use that to talk to them where they are. You can take the context you already know about their life (the more specific, the better) and make an educated guess about where people are on the pyramid path so you can help them along.

Only once someone's physiological and safety needs are taken care of can they begin to think about love and belonging, where they are focused on building relationships and community.

From there, respect and influence become important, including relevant status symbols like a nice car or house, and the final category of needs is about achieving your greatest potential and being completely fulfilled.

So, given what you know about your target customer, where are they focused on their own needs right now? What is the real problem these real people have that you can help solve?

If you get this right, this is like a superpower for your ability to communicate empathy in marketing anything. At its core, marketing is getting people's attention, and the best way to do that is to build long-term trust and respect with the empathy advantage.

If you're not sure where your Target Customer is focused currently... talk to them! You would be surprised (or perhaps not) at how few entrepreneurs actually do this. As Ray Edwards put it,[37]

"I used to play it as a joke and said you could actually talk to them. I'd say it, and I'd get a laugh. Now I say, 'But I'm serious. You actually need to talk to them.'

"So, I started calling people when the lockdowns began. I started calling customers out of our database at random. I didn't look at who is the biggest customer, who is the smallest, who has the least trouble, the most trouble, or any of those things. I just looked at who are we serving and what's going on with them. And I started asking...

"It's interesting because the first element that gets into the conversation is suspicion. 'Why are you calling me? Are you trying to sell me something?' And I would say, 'No, I'm just calling to see how it's going. What are you experiencing? We're trying to figure this out, too. So, talk to me about what's happening in your world, in your business.'

"And that level of communication, I realized we should have been doing this all along. Yeah. We should have been. Why were we not serving people at the highest level possible? And I think it's not because we didn't want to. We didn't realize what the highest level possible was until we were forced to come up with a new standard.

"Talk to your customers and really listen to them. Don't call with an agenda, don't call to sell them something, just call to find out where it hurts."

This hierarchy is a helpful tool at all times but becomes especially useful in response to a global crisis where nearly everyone has been knocked down to the bottom two rungs.

During COVID-19 and the simultaneous Great Lockdown and Great Reset, with millions at risk of infection and millions more unemployed, everyone hit a reset button on their climb up the pyramid to make sure they could stay healthy and pay their basic bills.

If you were selling something to help people reach their "full potential" (self-actualization) before the crisis, you're not selling that now. The same exact product may need to be repositioned so it addresses real problems that real people need solutions for right now.

Is Your Target Customer OPEN?

You probably know people who have serious problems you wish you could fix, but they don't seem to care or want your help as far as you can tell. That can be frustrating at family gatherings, but, in business, that's a death sentence you need to avoid.

Ray Edwards created a framework that is helpful for giving words to the reality that many customers are simply not aware of the problem you are out to solve.

You may have complete clarity about where your product relates to a customer's climb up Maslow's Hierarchy of Marketing, and you may have a clear description of how that translates into a very real transformation for your Target Customer, but it doesn't matter if your customer isn't aware that they need to transform!

This is where Ray's OPEN Buyer Awareness Scale comes in handy.[38] Every potential customer, at any moment, is at one of four levels of awareness of the problem that your product is designed to solve:

- **O**blivious: At this stage, customers are not even aware the problem exists. If you sell a nutrition supplement, these are the customers eating McDonald's every day who aren't concerned about their diet because they "feel fine."
- **P**ondering: At this stage, prospects are becoming aware of the problem and may be thinking about solving it in some way. Back to the drive-thru, this might be the prospect who starts to regret the Big Mac and McFlurry an hour later and is thinking they should start eating healthier as the indigestion turns into a sluggish lack of energy at work.
- **E**ngaged: This is when your prospect is actively seeking a solution to their problem. In the same example, maybe the person couldn't button their jeans today and is finally committed to making a change. They start texting friends and searching on Google to look for the best weight loss

smoothie recipe, including a nutritional supplement, so they can eat healthier today.

- **N**eed: Your prospect reaches this stage of awareness when they are absolutely desperate for a solution. In the same example, what if the prospect got blood work from their doctor that was dangerously unhealthy, and they had to lose weight this year or risk a heart attack? They would try anything and everything, including your product, desperate for an immediate solution.

You're wasting your time selling solutions to people in the "Oblivious" stage, and solving a problem for "Pondering" people is a poor use of your energy and time. You should not market your products to any prospects in the "Need" stage of awareness. If you do, you will come across as manipulative or needy, neither of which are good.

Instead, position your products as the perfect solution for anyone in the "Engaged" stage of awareness. These are the people you have the best chance of actually helping, leading to real transformation (a.k.a. satisfied customers) and customers in the "Need" stage will find you and buy from you all the same.

To be clear, the problem could be exactly the same with each person and just as severe. Awareness is a whole other animal and, for the most part, beyond your control. Major non-profits and policy groups spend massive amounts of money over decades to increase "awareness" for important issues, but it's a long, uphill climb.

To build a thriving business, focus on solving problems for real people who are aware of the problem in question and engaged in actively seeking a solution to that problem. That's the most direct route to influence that leads to transformative outcomes and income for you.

> *Claim your* **FREE business assessment**
> *($100 value) and unlock additional resources at*
> *YourThriveScore.com*

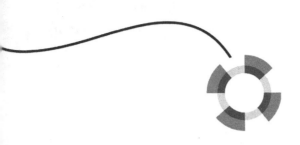

Chapter 3:

Sell Your Solution

Develop Opportunities for Prospects to Try What You Sell

By this point, you understand that your job as an entrepreneur is to solve a problem for a profit, and the fundamental decision you have made by now is which real people you will help and what real problem you will solve with your business.

All of those choices are necessary to get you to this point where you clarify the real solution that you will offer to real people (with real problems) and how you will market that real solution.

I use words like "real" when we talk about people, problems, or solutions because the internet has introduced a layer of separation between the entrepreneur and the customer that has led many well-meaning people astray, focused on numbers like "Subscribers" or "Followers" or even "Sales" without making the mental connection that there are real human beings on the other side of the transaction who fund the ongoing business endeavor.

Your real solution, then, needs to be practical and applicable, but it also needs to be a means to an end. You cannot bottle up and sell "Happiness" in a jar but you can (and should) offer real solutions that help people achieve happiness. In other words, your solution is always a means to an end.

People don't buy bandages so they can have small adhesive strips in their possession; they buy bandages to either stop bleeding or prepare to stop future bleeding and allow their body to heal.

People don't buy books (like this one) to have a bound collection of pages with words in their collection; they buy books to gain insight and understanding that allows them to become healthier, wealthier, or happier.

Similarly, you want customers to purchase your solution (or product), but to do so you must draw a clear connection between the solution you offer and the transformation your customer will receive.

The transformation you offer is the end goal of the infinite game that you play in (see *The Infinite Game* by Simon Sinek) or a milestone along the way. It may be far off or ultimately unattainable, but you must genuinely want to help your customers make progress along the way.

The real solution you offer is your product, your collection of products, or your plan. This is the path to transformation that you offer to customers, or potential customers, as a business.

Just as your real people (or target customer) can have a varying degree of specificity in how much you specialize to reach a certain niche group of people, so can your solution or plan.

In fact, the more you niche down with your target *people*, the less you need to niche down with your *solution*, and the reverse is also true.

For example, in the medical field, oncologists treat cancer (and within oncology there are even further degrees of specifically what type of cancer you choose to focus on). How they treat cancer varies wildly, not just from clinic to clinic but patient to patient. An oncologist can offer a myriad of treatment types including chemotherapy, thoracentesis, radiation, and pharmaceutical prescriptions of all types (just to name a few solutions).

Because the oncologist specializes in the type of people they serve (cancer patients), they can build a thriving business without specializing dramatically in the type of solution they offer to their group of people. If you have a very specific, life-threatening form of cancer, you're likely to pursue the most specialized oncologist available regardless of how expensive they are.

The reverse is also true. A deep tissue massage therapist chooses to specialize in a specific type of solution or plan and can attract a myriad of seemingly unrelated customers who all want the same treatment. Competitive athletes and corporate executives can both go to the same massage therapist seeking similar treatment, and the therapist can still build a thriving business because of the specialization in the solution offered at the end of the day.

Specializing in your target customer is best because that makes how you market and deliver your product or service much easier, especially in the Attention Economy where demand is much more important than supply.

Still, if you have only minor specialization in your target customer but you hyperspecialize in your product or service, then you still have a path to a thriving business.

The absolute best, the holy grail of business, is when you have a clear target customer and a clear niche product that can meet customer demand. With that type of business design, you can scale transformation (and profit) dramatically with little effort and very little time.

Still, some people struggle with narrowing their real people *and* their real solution, so I mention the tradeoffs to give perspective if you find it easier to specialize in either your target customer or target transformation rather than trying to specialize in both.

An Example of a Business Selling a Solution

Okay, let's dive into a specific example of a clothing store, perhaps a small boutique owned by a woman who enjoys fashion and has a small brick-and-mortar location in her town.

Just because of her location, she has already decided to limit her Target Customer to local people (for the sake of this example, let's assume her online presence is nonexistent or minimal in terms of actual sales).

Within the local subset of people, she has identified working women as the "Real People" she wants to serve. Of course, she is not going to hang a sign on her door that says "working women only" or turn away stay-at-home moms or men as customers. She simply has to pick one group to build her business around so she can come to understand their unique, specific needs.

With "Working women in Maury County" as her Real People, she starts talking to people she knows in that group and getting to know the problems they face on a regular basis (because of her existing preference, she is focusing on fashion or clothes).

Very quickly, she discovers that these working women have a real problem that she is fired up to solve. These working women complain that they struggle to find the right balance of professional clothing that still allows them to feel confident, feminine, and comfortable without either being too comfortable and casual or too stiff and masculine, so they stress out on a daily basis about what to wear to work.

At this point, our entrepreneur realizes that these problems are specific to the professional business office landscape, and she revises her target customer description to be "Women in Maury County who work in professional business environments."

At this point, she has clarity on the real people and the real problem, and she only needs a real solution to flesh out her business offer in her community.

First off, she takes stock of her current inventory and realizes that most of the products she sells are casual weekend wear; she only has a couple of outfits available that could be considered professional attire, so she reshuffles her layout and creates a dedicated section at the front of her store with a suite of business professional attire for women, all together in one place.

Secondly, she realizes that the products are simply a means to an end, because the ultimate transformation her target customer wants is the freedom to feel confident and classy at work. With this in mind, she offers a new "Working Woman's Wardrobe" service, where you can book a 90-minute appointment with her to get a personalized fitting and styling session and walk away with a full wardrobe of a half dozen confident and classy outfits appropriate for the workplace, all for a set fee of $2,500.

After a brief announcement about the new offer, a curious shopper tries it out and loves the outfits she takes home. She walks into the office with an extra dose of confidence each day and, within a month, she gets the promotion she was hoping for. Elated, she celebrates with her friends over a drink and tells them all about the "Working Woman's Wardrobe," so they go to the store to check it out.

Most of them aren't ready to spend $2,500 on a full experience, but they each find a dress, shirt, or blazer they like. Just like that, business is booming and word travels fast. If you're a working woman in the community, you know where you're going the next time you need to update your wardrobe.

Because the solution here is directly tied to transformation, there are some complementary product offerings that just make sense. The business owner could partner with a local dry cleaner to refer customers back and forth to each other, and free classes on "How to Negotiate Your Next Promotion" or "How to Be a Boss Lady in a Man's World" may make sense.

The key to success here is to get clear on the transformation you offer in terms of solving problems and the solution (or plan) you provide to help your customers achieve that transformation. Then your marketing communication, product offerings, and any free services you offer need to tie into that single transformation, even if the solutions you offer do vary a bit.

Ray Edwards provided another example how local massage therapists in his area adapted their business during the Great Reset because they chose to remain solution-focused:[39]

> "I've got a couple of friends who run massage therapy practices, and they are both doing online training, like videos, where you pay to get access to the video, and the video shows you how to self-massage. Because for a lot of people, it's not just a luxury. It feels good to get a massage; for me, it's physical therapy. I need it to function properly

because I have a neurological problem, so that's what brought that to mind for me. I contacted my practitioner and said, 'What are you going to be doing because I know we can't come in to get a massage?' She said, 'Well, I can show you these techniques.'

"And she talked about how she's going to do that online. She's also doing training by teaching massage therapists how to massage and the modality she uses to work with clients. And then offering ongoing membership payments so that during the time when things are back to normal, as close to normal as it can get, it normalizes her revenue stream by having people pay a monthly fee. And they get one massage a month at a discounted rate. And they can add on to that. So, whereas before, it was maybe catch as catch can, they would come in once every two, three months, or once every month and a half or so. Now they're scheduled like clockwork, and they don't miss it, and they actually end up buying more massages. So, I think this kind of thing applies to any business."

Sample Your Solution

Have you ever noticed how kids dash toward the free samples at Kroger or Costco from a mile away? They get the appeal. Even if you're not running (on the outside), you're probably curious to see what you're going to get for free.

If you like the sample, you may buy the full product—and even if you don't buy that specific product, you're more likely to buy more, buy more often, or both.

Common sense and experience explain this, but academic studies back it up. Dan Ariely, a behavioral economist at Duke University, explains that samples lead to sales for two reasons:

"What samples do is they give you a particular desire for something… If I gave you a tiny bit of chocolate, all of a sudden it would remind you about the exact taste of chocolate and would increase your craving."

As an added bonus, Ariely adds, "Reciprocity is a very, very strong instinct. If somebody does something for you, you really feel a rather surprisingly strong obligation to do something back for them."[40]

This strategy isn't limited to food and beverages; it works in many different industries.

Once you know the right prospects to pursue, you need to offer a clear sample solution that gives people a chance to tiptoe into transformation with your business. This could be a free download, some high-value content that doesn't require a huge investment or a sample version of your product itself.

You need to collect some kind of information, like a name and email address, to contact people in this group and nurture the relationship until they become paying customers.

Are you giving away free samples yet? Do you have a sample solution to your Target Customer's real problem freely available so they can try before they buy? Are you using this sample solution to reach new people or collect their contact information?

Your first job in business is to get people's attention, and it's not enough to tell people about your product. They need to experience it themselves.

Once you're clear on your Target Customer, step back a bit and identify what makes a good prospect, which is someone who could become a customer in time. The reality is every person on the planet is a prospect, but not all prospects are equal. Get clear on your Target Customer. When this is done, getting in front of the right people with the right information becomes clear.

Free Doesn't Mean Useless

Despite the fact that you're giving away free samples, you should treat this as a financial transaction. We live in the age of information where it seems like everyone has a free ebook or another download—so your free sample needs to stick out from the crowd. Allan Dib, CEO of Successwise and author of *The 1-Page Marketing Plan*, takes this approach:

> "I've got a rule where my free stuff should be better than other people's paid stuff. So, it's not just promote and sell, and all of that sort of stuff, as is often the case on people's mailing lists; I really treat that as a product. If someone was paying for this product, what kind of value would I want to deliver? So, there's that step up to the book, which sold for $2.99 on Kindle, and then another $10 or $14 for the paperback, whatever it's retailing for. Above that, I sell the course. So, it's basically taking the concept in the book and moving people through implementation."[41]

With that mindset, would your target audience pay for what you're giving away? If the answer is no, create a new sample solution. You need an irresistible offer, perhaps one that seems crazy to give away (this is not the same as a 10% off coupon).

Phillip Stutts, the founder of two marketing agencies and the author of *Fire Them Now*, took this advice to the bank,

> "So, we have given away all of our data that we have invested, at this point, $125,000 in. Each report is about

$25,000 of investment for us, and we have given it all away because we're trying to keep other business owners, who are willing to work with us, safe. When you are rooted in data, and you're not asking people for anything, that builds trust, and frankly, it's helping everybody we're giving it to. So, we've had over 94,000 downloads or data so far. Wow. Have we picked up a lot of clients out of that? Absolutely. But I gave first, I did not ask for anything. I did not say give me money first. We just decided to give first, and it's been crazy. So, that's how we did it. This was not a marketing plan. This literally was on March 5 when I asked myself a question: How do I want to be remembered a year from now? And I started writing, and I wrote for about an hour, and this was the one of the solutions I came up with."[42]

Your objective here is to get your first "Yes" and allow potential customers to sample what your business can offer, but it's also to create a direct connection between your sample solution and your standard solutions (your products).

How to Price Products Based on Transformation

Selling products would be much simpler if there was a simple equation that told you how much to charge, wouldn't it? But, of course, it's not that simple, and for a good reason. Price is simply an estimate of how much something is worth, and that varies from person to person and day to day.

That doesn't mean your prices should change every day, but consider bottled water as an example product. Generally, it costs a couple of dollars to get a bottle of water at a convenience store during checkout, but is that what it's worth?

Alternatively, you can buy a full case of water bottles and end up paying half the cost for a single bottle of water, but why does that price change matter? A bulk case of water bottles requires more plastic, in the form of the container surrounding the water bottles, yet the per-bottle cost is less.

That is because any company in their right mind charges the most they possibly can for a product while still making sales. If a convenience store could charge $1,000 for a case of water bottles and still make sales, they could and they should—but charging $1,000 for a case of water bottles would halt sales completely at the grocery store, at least for that brand.

Side note: That's why competitors are so healthy because the constant tug-and-pull between competitors on a balance of price and quality is what keeps market prices in check.

Back to the $1,000 case of water bottles. At the grocery store, that price doesn't make sense. But what if the environment changes? Speaking personally, if I were stranded on a desert island without a clean source of drinking water, I would happily pay $1,000 or more for a case of water bottles, and I bet you would do the same.

The supplies and materials required to make the case of water bottles are the same, but the price could be much higher (even if the water bottles were transported for free by a solar-powered drone).

What changes in each situation is not the cost of production or the amount of product, but the demand. This is what economists refer to as subjective value, which is how prices work in the real world.

There is no magic formula for pricing products based on how much they cost you to produce, or even the average price on the market. The perfect price is the highest price you can charge without losing your target customer to a competing company that is charging less.

Practically speaking, what does that mean?

Your cost to produce each product is irrelevant, except as a baseline you can never cross to make sure you cover your costs. The upside to your product prices is based on subjective value; how much is your product or service worth to your target customer?

To answer that question, it's important to remember that people don't consciously buy products; they buy the promise of a better version of themselves.

A water bottle is the promise of being less thirsty, unless you're stranded on an island where a water bottle is the promise of more life (hence, far more value).

When you look at your business, what transformation are you promising for sale? Do your products offer a faster, stronger, healthier, smarter, wealthier, or happier version of your customer's life? The more specific you can dial in this transformation, the more confidently you can charge a premium price.

That is why niche businesses are so lucrative in the new economy, where a single entrepreneur can take their products or services to a niche audience and sell more products to those people more often than a broad, general business with a bigger marketing budget and larger audience.

For example, I own a coworking space for entrepreneurs that has been modestly successful, and I foresee it will continue to grow steadily over the next decade and more.

By contrast, my friend (and therapist) Marcus Geromes started a coworking space just for licensed therapists and, after just a few years, Therapy Space now has hundreds of high-paying clients across a half dozen locations, all because they offered a similar amenity but to a much more specialized audience with very specific needs.

As you can see, being "niche" or specialized is a spectrum, not an on-and-off switch. Know your target customer enough to know how your products will change their life for the better, and you can charge for transformation.

So, what solutions will you offer? What plan or path for transformation will your business feature? Naturally, that means you need to clearly communicate the specific products you feature but always in the form of a real solution to a real problem that real people (your target customer) already have.

---

*Claim your **FREE business assessment** ($100 value) and unlock additional resources at YourThriveScore.com*

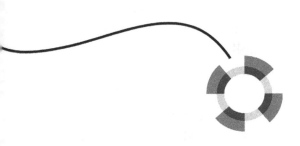

Chapter 4:

Court Your Customer

 t this point, you have made three important choices about your business model:

1. Your Real People (target customer)
2. Their Real Problem (your focus)
3. Your Real Solution (your plan or products)

That's all fine and dandy, but I'm sure you're itching to put these decisions to the test by actually building your business, which is about paying customers more than ideas on paper at the end of the day.

Have no fear, the next chapter will be fully focused on the five growth models you can pick from to grow your business (there are only five) and this chapter will walk you through a practical study of the mating ritual of a customer in the wild.

To be clear, mating is a metaphor, and there will be no sordid details about actual mating or anything truly wild here that you would not expect in a business book (unless you primarily read business textbooks, in which case this will be far more exciting than your typical read).

In the same way that young adolescents require education to prepare them for dating and marriage, entrepreneurs need to learn our own relationship options and the best path to success.

After all, that's the core of marketing in business: relationships. A business simply allows you to have relationships at scale, with hundreds or thousands (or millions) of customers. It may seem at first assessment to be a purely transactional relationship, but I do hope you will suspend your disbelief for a few minutes while I attempt to persuade you otherwise.

But first, a word about marketing feuds. There are, of course, many companies that use marketing to try and publicly jab at each other, but that's not what I am referring to. Instead, I would like to highlight a quiet feud behind the scenes of many companies where there are competing philosophies of marketing today.

There are many marketing philosophies that espouse building "brand awareness" or "engagement," and they are happy to spend seemingly unlimited amounts of time and money to do so, pointing back to any business success as due to marketing efforts in a roundabout way. Some even use the term "halo effect" to describe how one piece of marketing content (such as a Facebook ad) can drive sales for several different unrelated products as a byproduct of connecting to customers online.

As a traditionally trained economist, however, I was taught early on never to mistake correlation with causality.

Causality is direct cause-and-effect understanding where you can clearly follow the connection between the fact that when you fire an employee, they no longer work for you, or when you eat food with soy in it, you blackout for approximately forty minutes and wake up with what feels like a hangover (no, is that just me?).

Correlation comes from loose ties that are hard to explain directly and may, in fact, be completely unrelated, such as that more social media posts and more sales happen at roughly the same time or the fact that there is an inexplicable correlation between the number of people who drown annually by falling into a pool and the number of films that Nicolas Cage appeared in, in the same year. See the graph:

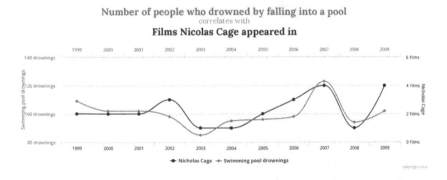

Number of people who drowned by falling into a pool
correlates with
Films Nicolas Cage appeared in

Yes, that last factoid comes from Spurious Correlations[43], a website and book project that a military intelligence analyst and Harvard Law student named Tyler Vigen published to illustrate the golden rule that "correlation does not equal causation." From the introduction to his book,

"In the late 1800s in Holland, a curious phenomenon occurred: The human birthrate rose at the same pace as the local population of white storks. Generations of parents would later rely on the connection to avoid awkward conversations with their children. While the story faded into folklore, the real-life correlation persisted. New research in the twentieth and twenty-first centuries has consistently confirmed a statistically significant connection between storks and human birthrates in a number of European countries.

"In 1958, William Phillips, a professor at the London School of Economics, published a paper regarding the connection between unemployment and inflation. As other economists explored Phillips' data, the correlation spread like wildfire: high inflation rates were linked to low unemployment and vice versa. The policy implications were explicit. National economies needed only to choose between inflation and unemployment, or somehow find a balance between the two. The Phillips curve, as the connection came to be called, informed macroeconomic policy decisions for years in both Europe and the United States.

"Humans are biologically inclined to recognize patterns. We spend thousands of dollars on college because education level correlates with monetary earnings later in life. We are attracted to the strong smell of freshly baked cookies because the strength of the aroma correlates with the proximity of the cookies. We go to bed early because a good night's sleep correlates with a better mood the next day."

Tyler goes onto explain that,

"Correlation, as a concept, means strictly that two things vary together. Automobile use correlates with automobile accidents. Warm weather correlates with ice cream sales. Overcast skies correlate with rain. But then there's this one: The number of films Nicolas Cage has appeared in each year correlates with the number of people who have drowned by falling into a swimming pool."

In terms of marketing philosophies, there is only one school of thought that focuses on causality over correlation, and that is direct response marketing.

A Direct Approach to Direct Response Marketing

Direct response marketing rose to fame in the 1960s[44] as a contrast to the "Mad Men" approach of massive ad campaigns to drive awareness and affinity for national brands. Beginning primarily with mail-order ads, direct response marketers set out to run campaigns to sell products exclusively where they could measure results, learn, and improve over time.

The beginning of direct response marketing can actually be traced back to Montgomery Ward, a U.S. merchant who published the first mail-order catalog in 1872. By 1888, he had built a business with $1,000,000 in annual sales (the equivalent of $21.8 million in 2020 dollars).[45]

Titans of marketing like Jay Abraham, Eugene Schwartz, and Robert Cialdini paved a path for internet marketing, before the internet existed, by planting a flag in the sand that every marketing campaign needed to be tracked, evaluated, and improved by metrics at the end of the day.

Print mail campaigns are still surprisingly effective, but most marketing energy has been redirected to the World Wide Web of the internet, with competing philosophies tagging along.

The reality is massive corporations like Coca-Cola[46] and Disney[47] can afford to run general brand awareness and affinity campaigns that cost them hundreds of millions of dollars without a clear line from ad to sale, but the average small business or startup entrepreneur can't and shouldn't do that.

 When every dollar counts, you need to count every dollar.

Brian Kurtz, one of the living legends who rode the wave from offline to online marketing, shared this explanation of modern Direct Response Marketing,

> "In direct marketing, it's a three-legged stool. It's your list, your offer, and your creative. The first step is you've got to have a list. When I start coaching a client or consulting with a client or working with my groups, I assess their assets. I go, what do you have? What do you have now? If you haven't done anything, you still have some stuff. And what I mean by that is you have a list, whether it's in an email distribution system, or it's a Facebook list, or it's just your email contacts, or you may have a bunch of postal addresses somewhere. The key is to get that list cleaned up and be able to assess that list in some way, with an offer, and the offer can be content."[48]

So, practically speaking, without getting a master's degree in Direct Response Marketing, what does this mean? I'm glad you asked!

Courting Your Customer with Direct Response Marketing

As promised, let's take a moment to evaluate the mating ritual of the average customer considering an everyday purchase such as a new pair of shoes. She wants to try something new that is both comfortable and professional enough to wear at the office, so she sends a text message to a coworker to ask, "Where did you get your shoes? I love the way they look! Are they comfortable? I'm thinking about getting a similar pair." In response, the coworker gladly recommends a downtown boutique and, after a quick Google search to find the place, our customer is delighted to see that the boutique offers a free guide to the perfect balance of comfort and fashion in professional shoes, so our customer provides her email address to get the free guide.

A week goes by and things have been busy, but it's finally Saturday and our customer has some time to herself. She is thinking about going downtown when she gets a notification; the boutique sent her an email that they are having a working women fashion show this afternoon!

Gleefully, the customer gets lunch with a friend and then they both go to the fashion show afterwards, cheering on the volunteer models and oohing and ahhing over each outfit presentation. After the brief show, our customer makes her first purchase at the boutique; she buys the $75 pair of shoes she had been considering, and she also buys a $80 dress she liked the look of after she saw a model wearing it who looked a lot like her.

That story is a fairly typical look at the buying process of the average customer, and it involves the customer going through three specific stages:

1. **The Prospect.** Technically speaking, everyone on the planet is a "prospect" in that they are a potential (or prospective) customer who could buy your products, but obviously some people are better prospects than others because they more closely align with your target customer description. A warm prospect is engaged in actively seeking a solution to a problem that you offer a solution to, so in this example the woman is a warm prospect when she thinks about getting new shoes and she texts her coworker friend.

2. **The Lead.** A prospect becomes a lead when they give their first "Yes" in response to an offer and, similarly, some leads are better than others based on how well they are "qualified" by the initial offer. Someone who follows your Instagram profile, for example, may technically be a lead because they said yes to follow you, but they are a minimally qualified or low-quality lead. In this example, the woman becomes a lead when she downloads the guide in exchange for her email address; she is a highly qualified lead because the offer was specifically about professional, comfortable shoes (which the boutique sells).

3. **The Customer.** Of course, this is where we want to be headed with the right target customer because a lead becomes a customer when they give you their first dollar bill. Similar to prospects and leads, there are varying degrees of quality and value in each customer because a customer who buys a $2 keychain is not as engaged with your business as the woman in this example, who spent $155 for some shoes and a dress.

All together, these three phases explain the customer journey and form a direct response marketing funnel for your business.

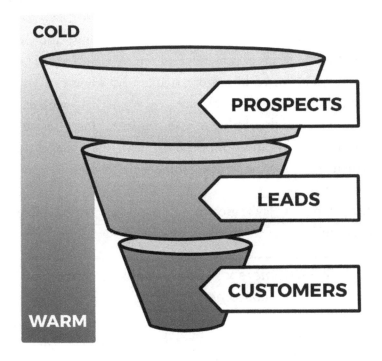

As prospects become leads and leads become customers, your business grows. In fact, Jay Abraham pointed out that there are only three ways to grow the revenue of any business:[49]

1. Increase the number of clients.
2. Increase the average transaction value.
3. Increase the frequency of repurchase.

Ray Edwards, another marketing legend and master copywriter, expounded on Jay's three-pronged growth strategy, saying,

"If you think about it, there's nothing you can do that really falls outside those three definitions of how to increase the revenue in your business. Right? And if you do any one of them, it helps. But if you do all three of those things, and even 10% more, it's multiplicative. It's not just additive. So, think in terms of how can I add more customers? How can I get them to buy more frequently? How can I get them to spend more each time they purchase with me? That increases their value to your business, increases your profitability, but most importantly, it increases the level at which you're serving your customers and clients."[50]

Let's look at Jay's growth strategy in action. Here's an application:[51]

1000 customers x $100 per sale x 2 sales per customer = $200,000

With a 10% increase in each variable, you get a 33% increase in total revenue:

1100 customers x $110 per sale x 2.2 sales per customer = $266,200

Communication, typically in the form of content, is how you warm up people within each stage of your funnel to keep them increasingly engaged. In direct response marketing, we call this "copy." As Ray Edwards explains,[52]

"Nora Ephron said everything is copy, and I've believed that for a long time. I've never been more adamant about it than I am now. Everything. Every communication you have in your business, whether it's what you say, when you answer the phone, what's on your business card, what's on your website, what's in your emails, what's in your ads, what's on your sales pages, what's in your checkout pages—it's all copy.

"And what I mean by that is you're always making a sale: You're just selling people on you and your business, or you're selling them on the competition because you're not doing a great job. You're not connecting with them.

"[The] quality of your business is equal to the quality of your communication. And the quality of your communication is equal to its clarity and its relevance to the person you're communicating with."

At each milestone in your funnel, however, you need more than content. You need a clear offer that customers can respond to in the form of a yes or no. If yes, some offers will be free (or financially free but require an exchange, such as providing an email address). Other offers will cost money, and some should cost very little so as to be painless, while others can and should cost a whole lot more.

Anytime a customer says no to an offer (which may simply mean they didn't respond), what they are saying could either mean "Not for me" or simply "Not yet."

The more closely your prospect, lead, or customer aligns with your Target Customer, the more likely they should be to say yes to your offers, but the reverse is also true.

The less closely aligned your prospect, lead, or customer is to your target customer, the more likely they should be to say no! To be clear, your marketing should act exactly like a magnet—and, by the way, magnets do two things.

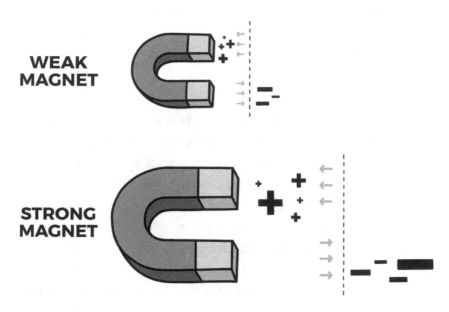

Magnets attract and repel energy in roughly equal strength. They attract the right energy and repel the wrong energy, but weak magnets allow the wrong energy to get close to them without resistance, while strong magnets both attract the right energy from a distance and keep the wrong energy far, far away.

So, you may be wondering (or perhaps you forgot), how does this relate to mating and dating? Well, your job as a business owner is to identify people who are looking for a solution, attract them to your business with your content, and then ask them out. That's the first "yes" of becoming a lead; in your business relationship, that's like the first date. You're likely to get many more suitors in the form of high-quality leads if you start with a date rather than jumping straight to the sales process with a "Hi, we just met, but will you marry me? Or at least sleep with me?"—which is how direct sales come across.

Once you've got a lead (they said yes to the date), you have the chance to romance them with more offers (a second or third date). Once they're thoroughly invested, you can "make a move" to ask them to make a purchase and become a paying customer (perhaps even marrying you by purchasing your continuity membership product).

To recap from a previous chapter, to generate profit, you have to get people's attention (marketing) and persuade them to purchase your solution (sales) while simultaneously managing the incoming and outgoing dollars to end the day with more than you started (finance).

Direct response marketing is the frame that fits marketing and sales together, connecting the dots between the real people you serve with real solutions to their real problems and generating real revenue for your business.

My Socially Awkward Answer to Social Media

Whenever I work with a client who knows they have a marketing problem, their first question is about their social media strategy. Whether we're talking about how many followers they have on Instagram or how well their Facebook ads are performing, social media gets an undue amount of attention (at least while I'm writing this, in the year 2020).

Don't get me wrong, social media is a phenomenal innovation, a tool to create digital gathering places for like-minded people to connect and interact online. Like the cafe or pub of the past, social media has become the go-to community center for meeting new people or learning new ideas. As an entrepreneur, social media is a valuable tool in your toolbox (or more accurately, a category of tool, as each specific platform is different in its function and form).

Still, every time I work with a client who knows they have a marketing problem, their first question is about their social media strategy. When I dig a little deeper, I almost always find a massive, untapped opportunity in terms of their email list and search engine traffic that is being mostly ignored. In fact, research shows that email subscribers are more likely to make a purchase than social media followers, and answering people's questions as they ask them (via search results) is far more effective than interrupting their Instagram exploration with an intrusive ad.[53]

So why do we spend so much time focusing on, and talking about, social media?

I believe it's because we have a visibility bias.

Right now, if you want to grow your business, it's natural to look around and wonder what other, more successful companies in your industry are doing (or perhaps companies outside your industry that you admire). The problem is, you don't have access to their email list to see what their open rates, click-through rates, or total subscriber counts are. You can see where they rank in search results for specific topics, but you can't see exactly how many people land on what pages or how many become customers quickly and quietly without a share, comment, or like on social media.

All you can see is what happens on social media. Even then, you can't see direct messages, but you can see that people post content, some people comment on it and others like it and share it, and you see their business success. Just as correlation does not mean causality with Nicolas Cage and swimming pool deaths, the correlation you see of success and social media does not mean that is the cause.

And yet, we are human. So, we try to copy what other people are doing but because of our visibility bias, we focus on what we can see, even if and when the unseen marketing efforts are actually driving the majority of sales.

Personally, I deleted my social media accounts, except for LinkedIn.[54] I don't recommend that approach for everyone, but I did that as an experiment inspired by Cal Newport's book *Digital Minimalism*, and I haven't looked back.

For clients, or even my own businesses, I use social media when I have a clear strategy on what it's meant for, but I use social media like Brian Kurtz, who explains, "Social media, to me, is a way to get people on my email list. And once they're on my email list, I romance them."[55]

When Should You Publish Your Price?

Remember, in the Attention Economy the consumers have the power. Because of the internet, consumers have direct access to a dozen other possible solutions to their problems besides yours, and they have access to limitless information if they decide to solve their problems on their own.

Your product, and your business, is on trial. You have a limited window to make your case as to why people should buy your solution from you, right now. While it's true that you should court your customer along the path from prospect to lead to customer without rushing them along, you may not notice the moment that your courting pays off, and they've fallen in love!

Rather than negotiate prices with each customer, make sure you have clearly visible price points for versions of your real solution at drastically different prices.

Once upon a time, your business could say "Contact us for pricing" or display products without a price, and still expect a sale, but you are no longer a gatekeeper. Your customer is looking for a simple, painless purchase process and one of the first questions they have is probably price.

That doesn't mean price is the only factor, so I'm not advocating rock bottom prices for any of your products, but just the clarity of a clear, unapologetic price tag will save you and your potential customer a lot of energy and time.

If an engaged prospect visited your business right now, what is the most amount of money you would allow them to spend?

The first time I heard that question, I was as confused as you may be right now. Allow them to spend? Why, everything of course!

But what if you aren't readily available and you can't create a custom offer on the spot? What if a customer visits your website or walks into your store while a junior employee is at the front desk?

Are you offering enough transformation, in the form of clearly communicated offers for solutions, at all times? What kind of painless purchase can you offer where you can exceed the customer's expectations tenfold and make it easy for them to say yes with a dollar attached?

Once you have clearly visible pricing for drastically different priced products (priced based on the promised transformation of each), you have a pricing strategy that will serve you well.

---

*Claim your **FREE business assessment** ($100 value) and unlock additional resources at YourThriveScore.com*

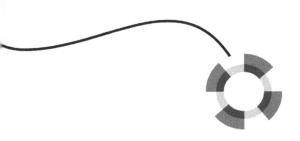

Chapter 5:

Choose Your Path

Select a Primary Growth Model to Accelerate Your Results

n 2019, I had the exciting opportunity to serve as master of ceremonies for Michael Hyatt's event, The Focused Leader, alongside my friend Neal Samudre as co-emcee. Naturally, I was thrilled! But… I found out only two weeks before the actual event.

I always get compliments when I wear my light blue blazer, so I decided to order the pants that go with it and turn it into a complete blue suit. I found the pants online and ordered them with expedited shipping (picking my size based on the jeans I wear on a normal, daily basis—big mistake).

The pants arrived a few days before the event, so I took them to a seamstress who promised fast service to get them hemmed. I walked into the dressing room, put on the pants, and… discovered they were about six sizes too small!

I couldn't come *close* to buttoning the pants. I showed them to the seamstress, and she shook her head; it would take double the amount of fabric to make the pants fit.

Of course, it was too late to reorder the pants in the correct size, so I called a friend, drove to Nashville, and got fitted for a brand-new suit.

After a week's worth of stress and a half-day of driving around Nashville, my suit was perfect—but I could have avoided that entire experience if I'd stopped to take measurements first.

How many times have you done the same thing with your business? Are you posting on social media or paying for advertising before you've stopped to ask if the pants even fit?

In the bestselling book *The Lean Startup*, Eric Ries identifies two core "Leap of Faith" assumptions that every business owner makes. The first is the "Value Hypothesis," which assumes your product delivers value to the customer in some way (for our purposes, this is the solution you settled on selling in chapter 3).

The second is the "Growth Hypothesis," which assumes new customers will find the product and revenue will grow. For your business to succeed, your assumptions about both value and growth need to be accurate. That's why you need to identify the assumptions you're making and find creative ways to test these with your target audience.

What is your plan to get in front of your target customer? Do you have a clear step-by-step strategy along with a way to track your results at each step?

Even though there are thousands of tactics you can try on hundreds of platforms, thankfully there are only five fundamental growth models in modern business.

How to Establish a Measurable Marketing Model for Growth

At this point, you know who your target customer is, and you know you need to court them to move them through your direct response funnel from prospect to lead to customer, so you've done important, foundational work to shore up your marketing capabilities. Now all you need to do is to run people through your funnel, which means you need a flood of incoming prospects to serve!

So, where do these people come from? Unfortunately, "build it and they will come" only works in the movies, so you need to establish a measurable marketing model that provides key metrics along the way; metrics that tell you if you're on the right track.

Do you know where your customers came from last month?

Once you know which of your marketing efforts are driving results, you can make better decisions. Do more of what works, less of what doesn't, and measure your marketing experiments.

Thankfully, there are only five growth models to choose from, but you do need to choose a single, primary growth model to focus on so you can get good at it and see your results with clarity.

Coming out of the Age of Information (into the Age of Insight), you have access to nearly limitless data—but without clarity on which metrics to actually focus on, which is what gives you the insight you need to optimize, thrive, and grow.

In *The Lean Startup*, Eric Ries identifies three growth models that startups rely on to consistently grow. I've identified two more growth models in today's marketing landscape, which are each a unique hybrid of the original three. Pick one primary growth model, and that clarity will help you narrow your focus to just tracking the data that matters to your business growth.

1. Viral Growth: Leverage Word of Mouth Marketing

The word "viral" has come to mean many things. Recently, viral may have lost its appeal as a goal given the global spread of the novel coronavirus, but that type of contagion is exactly the model for this type of person-to-person growth model (without the wheezing, hospitalization, or death).

In this case, growth can be viral, even on a small scale, by word of your business or products spreading from one person to another.

Also called "word of mouth" marketing, this model depends on people talking about, recommending, and sharing your business with the world. This model shows up in small-town business communities, big cities, and all over the internet (that's how organic social media already works).

Whenever one person shares your content, offer, or product with another, you get to borrow (temporarily) a bit of the goodwill built up in the relationship between those two people. You trust a recommendation from your close friend more than a stranger flipping a sign on the roadside, because you've built up a level of trust for your friend.

If this is your growth model, you need to be focusing on creating a phenomenal product, along with informative content that tells a compelling story. Good branding makes it easy for your customers to tell their friends about what you have to offer, so they can go check it out.

This is how Warby Parker rose to fame, seemingly out of nowhere. They provided beautiful eyeglasses, with a painless buying experience, that were so good that people kept telling their friends. Do you know people who wear Warby Parker? If so, they've probably told you (not so for people wearing Walmart glasses!).

When you're focused on viral growth, you may want to look for opportunities to incentivize people sharing your content or product with other people, and track metrics like shares or public reviews most of all.

Dropbox did this incredibly well early on, creating an onboarding process for new customers where they could "Get More Space" by following an easy-to-use interface to invite their friends to use Dropbox as well. This worked incredibly well, creating an army of customers working tirelessly to grow Dropbox; an army that grew in size as each wave of new referrals signed up.

Between September 2008 and January 2010, Dropbox skyrocketed from one hundred thousand to four million registered users (that's 3900% growth in just fifteen months). They've since surpassed five hundred million registered users—or one in fifteen people alive on the planet.[56]

At the time, Viral Growth was a logical choice for the Dropbox team because cloud storage was still a new concept, foreign to many people, and they knew it was only going to catch on if people developed the habit of using the platform together.

2. Paid Growth: Invest to Scale with Advertising

How much would you pay for ads if you knew that every $1 investment led to a $2 return? Obviously, as much as you could!

That's the big, bold promise of modern-day advertising, with deeply detailed targeting technology available, such as ads on Facebook, Google, and elsewhere on the web. Even billboards are making a comeback in the competitive war for attention today.

Successful Paid Growth is focused on tracking your Return On Ad Spend (ROAS) closely, which requires attention to detail and a mind for data because of the plethora of data available. Essentially, it comes back to one core question:

Are you getting more money out than you're putting in?

If the answer is yes, you can scale your campaigns to grow your business, but Paid Growth isn't magic.

Wicked Reports analyzed $1.5 billion in Facebook advertising, and discovered that the average Facebook advertising campaign lost money in 2018![57] On average, each campaign starts with a negative 82% ROI and takes four months to reach a negative 50% ROI.

That means that on average, after four months, people are making $1 for every $2 invested (a.k.a. a bad deal). Even if you reach a positive ROI, you have to manage cash flow closely, because you typically pay for ads before you see the results.

Still, Paid Growth works well for many companies, including the meal prep service Blue Apron—who you've probably heard sponsoring a podcast or offering a discount or free trial somewhere in your newsfeed. Paid Growth appears to be their primary growth model, and the same is true for many other businesses today.

If you're going to pursue Paid Growth, then perhaps the most important distinction to make first is whether you plan to market based on identity or intent (kudos to Joseph Bojang for introducing me to this concept).

Identity-based advertising reaches your Target Customer based on who they are or their demographics. This might include age, gender, income, location, or any other range of metrics available. Social media platforms like Facebook and Instagram are built for identity-based marketing, so if you are marketing an identity, those platforms are probably where you should start.

Intent-based advertising instead reaches your Target Customer based on actions they take, such as viewing your sales page or following a competitor's website or searching "How do I fix a leaky faucet?" on Google. Google is the king of intent-based advertising, along with the second most popular search engine in the world, YouTube, which is also owned by Google.

3. Sticky Growth: Develop Irreplaceable Infrastructure

Sticky Growth is difficult to pull off, but if you get it right, you create a business where every single customer is going to stay with you for years and pay a growing collection of fees.

Essentially, you can leverage Sticky Growth when you create products that become irreplaceable infrastructure somewhere in your customer's life. These are products with a high "switching cost," where happy customers aren't likely to leave.

The company that's done this the best is probably QuickBooks, which has become synonymous with "accounting software" and is the backbone of so many companies that they can't fathom ever making a switch.

Once you have an invoicing process, years of accounting history, along with budgets and forecasting all within the same platform, you've stopped actively considering alternative solutions. It doesn't matter if someone presents you with an option that has more features or even a lower price, you're stuck. QuickBooks would have to have a major breach in trust for you to consider switching, such as a data hack, a massive price hike for existing customers, or manipulating data.

If you can tap into Sticky Growth, you can afford to invest money in direct phone sales or expensive brand awareness projects, without a time-specific offer, to generate sales. You can take your time making each sale because the real value comes in over the long-term investment of each customer you serve. In fact, I would argue that Sticky Growth is the one growth model where indirect, brand awareness marketing is appropriate (although depending on the situation, it may still not be preferred).

Sticky Growth is incredibly difficult to pull off as a primary growth model, but if you can pull it off, it's as close as you're going to get to guaranteed long-term success. What many businesses do to take advantage of this is to select another growth model as their primary focus but build a secondary Sticky Growth model into their back end, flagship or complementary products for repeat customers.

Casey Graham built his company Gravy to be sticky by setting up a failed payment recovery service with clients who have recurring revenue businesses and charging a commission on recovered payments (so there was little risk to hire them, and a lot of potential upside). During the Great Reset, Casey got to feel the benefits of sticky growth firsthand when they only lost one, single customer (and gained quite a few at the same time). As he said,[58]

"Okay, we're sticky! We're in the revenue stream; we're adding value to these businesses—like, we always wondered, are they gonna fire us first? Because the number one thing everyone is asking is, is this essential? Yeah. So, we passed, and because of that, we doubled down, and that's why we've added 17 people in the last 90 days to our team, and we're really going to try to grow this thing."

4. SEO Growth: Rely on Robot Referrals

Search Engine Optimization, or SEO, is a growth strategy focused on becoming the source of key information your Target Customer is already searching for.

I like to think of this as an adapted form of Viral Growth, where you're relying on robots—not people—to refer your business as the solution. Google is the dominant search engine, but your Target Customer may also be searching on Pinterest, YouTube, Amazon, or elsewhere.

Have you ever noticed how Wikipedia shows up as the #1 or #2 website for almost any search on Google? That's because they've become the internet's encyclopedia, and you need to do the same thing for your industry-specific content to reach your Target Customer when they're searching.

Focus on optimizing in-depth content to become a niche publication, creating content that's so good other people will link to you. That, plus linking to your content, shows the robots you've got content worth seeing and sending people to.

Marcus Sheridan's book *They Ask, You Answer*[59] is perhaps the best available resource on this topic. He lays out a simple-to-implement content marketing model based on the massive success he had with River Pools and Spas during the Great Recession in 2008. By creating freely available content in direct response to every question customers had ever asked, Marcus built a massive library of genuinely helpful content that—somewhat by accident—ranked highly in search engines in response to specific, detailed questions their Target Customer was already searching for online.

5. Affiliate Growth: Pay People to Send You Customers

Growing your business with an affiliate network is a hybrid of both Viral Growth and Paid Growth because it involves other people talking about your product or business on your behalf, but money also changes hands.

The biggest difference between Affiliate Growth and Paid Growth is that with affiliates, you only pay a commission after you've seen the results.

If you already have Superfans talking about your product, this can be a great way to incentivize them to spread the word further. Develop relationships with a core network of affiliates who can promote you in exchange for a percentage of each sale they refer to you.

This model is how ConvertKit established themselves in a highly competitive market before they were known for their core software product or feature set. At the time, with a dozen massively successful email marketing software platforms on the market with well-established brands, the idea of bootstrapping a basic email marketing software seemed ludicrous, but Nathan Barry did it.

Even before ConvertKit had the best feature set on the market, they had the best relationships. They listened to their Target Customer, the content creators, and created features directly in response to their demand. This won them initial loyalty and trust long enough for those creators to spread the word about ConvertKit with their high-paying affiliate program that paid affiliates 30% of every sale from any referred customer, as long as that referred customer continued to pay.

That affiliate program was instrumental in their early success and still drives a third of their company revenue today.[60]

ConvertKit's secondary growth model was their Sticky Growth because email marketing software (with opt-in forms, downloads, and automated sales sequences) is at the core of many of these Creators' businesses. The idea of switching away from ConvertKit to another competitor was almost unthinkable once the customers were on board.

That combined growth strategy allowed ConvertKit to grow from Nathan Barry's side project to a massive software company that has hit the Inc. 5000 list of the fastest-growing privately held companies in America for three years in a row.[61] ConvertKit is part of an open startups initiative that shares their live numbers publicly, so as I write this, I can share that ConvertKit's annual recurring revenue is more than $23 million.[62] So they're doing something right!

Of course, you have to have a good product to achieve consistent success with Affiliate Growth because your affiliates are putting their reputation on the line to recommend whatever you have to offer. After that, most of the work involved with an Affiliate Growth model is in the relationships you develop with potential affiliates, active affiliates, and top affiliates as you provide them with resources to promote your product to their audience. This model relies on the principle in *7 Habits of Highly Effective People* to "Think win-win."[63]

Which Growth Model Will You Use?

The key to success is to focus on one measurable marketing model and dial that in, whichever growth model you choose. Any of these models could be the key to your success.

There is no shortage of opportunity today, but there is a shortage of execution. Stay focused, my friend. Which of these measurable marketing models do you think fits your business best?

Claim your **FREE business assessment**
($100 value) and unlock additional resources at
YourThriveScore.com

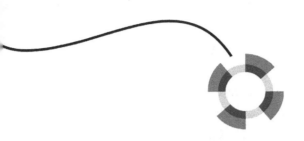

Chapter 6:

The Selling Story

Connect Your Products in the Narrative of a Sales Sequence

I used to hate buying new razors.

I would walk down the shaving and self-care aisle with a firm look on my face as if I knew exactly what I was looking for, but I didn't.

I would find a pack of razors that looked about right, or occasionally try a fancy one with a replaceable head, and then buy an overpriced bottle of some cream designed to make sure I didn't totally destroy my face.

If you've met me, you may find that surprising. Not that I had trouble picking out razors but that I even shave at all! I'm thirty, but I look like I'm about fifteen on a good day (I am reminded of this often by well-meaning strangers).

Regardless, I do shave my face on a regular basis, and that requires new razors on a regular basis, a buying process I never enjoyed… Until I met Dollar Shave Club.

In Dollar Shave Club's viral YouTube video about their product, they made a simple promise: They would send me a simple razor, for a simple price, on a regular basis. Stress-free shaving was mine! And I was sold.

Of course, while I was ordering my new razor, I discovered that the $1 razor that gave them their name was only the first option; they also had a mid-range and high-end razor (but only those three options that I could see).

I consider myself a middle-of-the-road guy (like most people), so I picked the mid-tier $5/month razor and, with that one choice, I kept getting new razor blades on a regular, automatic basis for the next seven years. Conservatively, I've spent nearly $1,000 with Dollar Shave Club (including both their core razor and complementary products), mostly without giving each purchase a thought.

How did this happen, and how can you create similar customer interactions with your business and brand? The answer isn't a viral YouTube video (although that can help). The answer lies within the story of how your customers interact with your products over the course of time.

Remember, the only way to grow your business is to sell more products to more people more often (or some combination of those three).

The not-so-secret path to pulling off all three of those is to build a sales sequence into your business model, so the path from one purchase to the next is as simple and painless as possible. I call this the selling story because this is not about creating limited-time offers or fancy pricing gimmicks to trick your customer into buying; this is about empathy.

Using empathy, you need to develop a product selection that solves problems within your customer's life so that your products are natural ingredients to the story of their ever-evolving life. Of course, that means a prerequisite to a supercharged sales sequence is to have a clear target customer (see chapter 2), but it doesn't stop there.

Once you have a rich, personal understanding of your target customer, you have work to do.

Offer a Clear Gateway Product

Once you have clarity on your target customer's problems, you need to identify a gateway product that solves your customer's painful problem.

Getting that first dollar from your customer is a huge milestone because people value their money, and it takes a leap of faith, to some extent, for people to pay for what you have to offer.

You can make that leap of faith as risk-free as possible, turning it into a step of security, by offering a low-priced gateway product your customers can use.

This product needs to provide real-life value and transformation but on a small scale (something like one simple shave). The price of the product is relative, depending on the type of customer you're serving and the range of prices your other products will cost.

If your average customer transaction is $10,000, then a $1 gateway product is probably too low.

If your average customer transaction is $50, however, then $1 or $2 is probably just about right.

There is no magic formula for this pricing; it is more art than science, but this is about psychology. In the mind of your Target Customer, what is a painless price point to take a chance on solving a real-life problem your customer has? For Dollar Shave Club, this was their $1 razor.

As another example, let's say you're running a women's clothing boutique. It's probably risky for me to pick that example, given my relative ignorance on women's clothing, but let's give it a shot!

As a women's clothing boutique, you're not selling hats, belts, and dresses. You're selling women a more confident, attractive version of themselves.

That's what they're looking for, and your target customer is hoping you have the product that is going to solve their problem of a wardrobe with dozens of outfits, but none they want to wear.

So, what could you offer as a gateway product? It could be a single pair of comfortable, classy shoes guaranteed to look good with nearly any outfit for a dash of daily beauty.

You could even share the research that most people notice your shoes upon a first impression before any other article of clothing (which, for some reason, is true).[64]

That one pair of shoes may cost $10 or $20 and won't fund your whole business, but it is a clear gateway product for a literal step of security your target customer can take (a quick Google search confirms that, yes, I went out on a limb with this example since women's shoes are never that cheap).

Once you've selected your gateway product, make sure it is featured prominently in your business, both online and in your physical storefront (if you have one). What you've just done is make the first purchase from a customer much easier because they don't need to waste energy wondering "Where should I start?"

Of course, some customers will skip your gateway product and go straight for the racks of options to pick their favorite, but many people want the simple solution (and even people looking for options have your gateway product as a reference point while they shop).

Develop a Flagship Product

If you have a customer go "all in" with your brand, love your products, and want to experience total transformation, what is the best option available to them?

Is the answer to fill their bags with more of your products? That sounds overwhelming and becomes more of a to-do list than an exciting transformation your target customer can experience.

That is why you need to develop a flagship product. Your flagship product is the epitome of everything you have to offer, the total transformation package, for a single premium price.

For Apple, this is their iPhone, which by itself drives more than 44% of annual revenue and also fuels another 18% of Apple's annual revenue in the form of apps sold on Apple's App Store and Apple Music subscriptions.[65]

For Dollar Shave Club, this is actually built into their name; their core razor is their flagship product—but they sell many complementary products that go along with their razor, such as a Traveler bath bag (and yes, I did buy it).

Cleverly, when I bought the Dollar Shave Club travel bath bag, it came with all these empty pockets and slots for other products I didn't quite have. It felt satisfying to put my razor in its designated slot, but I had lots of empty space until I bought deodorant, body soap, shaving cream, and aftershave to fill out the rest.

I even bought lip balm and body wash from Dollar Shave Club because they all fit together as part of a single flagship product with all my bathroom self-care needs!

Yes, they solve all your bathroom self-care needs, as they are proud to share that their "One Wipe Charlies" are a popular add-on to your Dollar Shave Club subscription when you're ready for a full immersion experience of their brand...   .

Now back to the women's boutique example. Flagship products are an under-utilized strategy in brick-and-mortar retail and are almost never offered.

A flagship product isn't just your more expensive product; it's a total immersion experience (one that, ideally, also promotes related sales of products that all naturally connect).

If you owned a women's clothing boutique, you could offer a "Working Woman's Wardrobe" as a flagship product for sale. In this experience, you would book a 90-minute appointment with a stylist to get a personalized fitting and styling session where you walk away with a full wardrobe of a half dozen confident and classy outfits appropriate for the workplace, all for a set fee of $2,500 (this is the example from chapter 3).

Rather than sell dozens of articles of clothing, you would be selling a flagship product of a single, transformative experience that happened to include dozens of articles of clothing and a built-in service fee.

Can you see how a flagship product could double the sales in your business, even with just a few individuals purchasing a flagship product each month?

And for those customers who never purchase the flagship product, they are still paying attention. They may buy more individual products without balking at the price tag simply because they are purchasing mid-tier products, rather than your flagship product at a premium price.

Cultivate a Continuity Product

A gateway product and a flagship product are key products to offer as real solutions to real problems for real people, but the crowning achievement in any business, that creates a stable foundation for long-term, thriving success, is a Continuity Product.

As John Warrillow makes the case in *The Automatic Customer*,[66]

> "Massive companies like Amazon, Apple, and Microsoft are adopting the subscription model to tighten their already firm grip on our wallets."
>
> So what? Why should you care? Your company doesn't have a hundred billion dollars in revenue, nor are you some start-up backed by venture capital.
>
> Did you pick up the wrong book? No.
>
> I think Mike McDerment, CEO and cofounder of the subscription business FreshBooks, said it best when we spoke about the subscription business model back in 2014: "It's the best da** business model in the world… it's got great predictability for planning, which helps you as an entrepreneur sleep at night."[67]

John is not alone in this assessment, either. As Allan Dib, author of *The 1-Page Marketing Plan*, puts it:[68]

> "One of the things I always look for, whether I'm investing in a business or I'm running the business is… is there a recurring revenue component?

"There's nothing more difficult in my view than starting the new month with revenue being at zero, right? And then, okay, now we've gotta hustle, we've gotta push, we've gotta cold call—all of that sort of stuff.

"So, I like knowing I can start the month and there's a minimum amount of recurring revenue that's going to come in. That's really, really powerful."

Similarly, I've worked with clients with six-figure or seven-figure membership sites that serve tight niche audiences and are rewarded with superfans who automatically pay the business for continued access, month after month.

The success of continuity, subscription-based products is more about the day-to-day growth and retention than a massive, fancy launch, so they are a lot less glamorous than one-time product launches, but they are a lot more reliable. I like to compare the growth model for Continuity products to stairs, rather than spikes, that require a long-term commitment to climb.

To be clear, continuity products take a lot of work to launch, grow, and manage, so they're typically not the best place to start. Still, once you can offer a continuity product to your customers, you can take the pressure off of your sales and increasingly focus on service, which is better for you and better for your customers, truly a win-win.

Thinking back to our women's clothing store example, that may seem like an industry where continuity products wouldn't work. To be fair, I don't visit women's boutiques often, but I've never seen one offer a subscription product—that doesn't mean they couldn't!

With the right clarity of customers and a focus on providing real solutions to real problems for real people, the path to transformation through a continuity product becomes clear. Let's assume the Target Customer for this business is a woman working in a professional business environment, similar to an earlier example in chapter 3.

What solutions does this Target Customer require on a regular—perhaps weekly or monthly—basis? What regular recurring problems do they have? Well, with a quick bit of research or a real-life conversation (yes, customers are people you can talk to), you might discover a list of regular recurring real problems your real people have:

- Too busy to keep up with any mending that their wardrobe needs
- Frustrated with the male-dominated workplace, and feeling held back
- Overwhelmed with the double life of caring for kids and home while also working
- Feeling uncomfortable or uninspired in their clothes a few months after purchase

Any one of these, or a combination, could be an inspiration for a continuity product. If this was your business, you could offer a subscription warranty service that guaranteed repair or replacement for any clothes bought from your store, or you could host a monthly discussion group (online or in-person) with guest speakers for women in the workforce to share guidance on breaking the glass ceiling or managing life at home while succeeding professionally at work.

Looking over these options, you may realize that the reason your customers are uncomfortable after a few months is that seasons change, and their wardrobe should change with it. Going back to your flagship product customers, you could offer a quarterly wardrobe refresh for $1,000 (styling included) and they would gleefully sign up.

Don't you see how when you're committed to serving real people, the long-term impact you can have on their life becomes foundational to your success with a continuity product?

What Is Your Selling Story?

In your target customer's life, how do your products fit together into a cohesive selling story that is both believable and clear?

Your gateway product and your flagship product exist at two ends of the spectrum, with your continuity product as the long-term commitment. But where do your products fit into the selling story? Do you even need other products?

Simply put, no. A gateway product and a flagship product are sufficient to build a thriving business, with a continuity product as the massive cherry on top. Still, depending on your industry and your passions, you may find it natural to add other products or services, and you can and should do that if you can fulfill those products without detracting from your core focus products.

Often, business owners make the mistake of carrying more products without thinking through the selling story, hoping that because the products are available, they are naturally going to sell.

As a matter of fact, the reverse may be true. If you are carrying products that your Target Customer doesn't want, you send a subtle signal that questions whether you "get them" and know what they need.

So, you have your gateway product and your flagship product. Let's assume you have a continuity product too. What other products does your customer need? First things first, make sure you're creating products to serve as real solutions to real problems for real people (and the right people), rather than just stuff to sell.

As you're considering more products in your selling story, there are only two categories of products other than your gateway, flagship, and continuity products worth consideration:

- Complementary products
- Supplementary products

Complementary products are natural, positive add-ons to your gateway product or flagship product that improves your customer's overall experience, for a fee. For Chick-fil-A, these are the waffle fries that naturally complement the classic chicken sandwich, but they've become so popular as a complement to any entree, or even a standalone product, that they are Chick-fil-A's most-ordered menu item overall![69]

Supplementary products are optional replacements to your gateway product or flagship product, typically because they are better or cheaper alternatives (but not both), or appeal to a nuance in customer preference. For Chick-fil-A, an example supplementary product would be their spicy chicken sandwich, which is not a top-selling product; but for many customers, its flavor is preferable to the classic chicken sandwich, strips, or nuggets that all have a similar taste.

In the services world, there are many different ways to present a solution in different formats for different prices, as either complementary packages or supplementary alternatives to your core offering. For example, Scott Beebe set up service packages at Business On Purpose this way:[70]

"We have a do-it-yourself level; we've got a do-it-with-others level. So, a DIY, DIWO… we have a do-it-with-us level; it's kind of our third tier—DIWU. And then we have a done-for-you [that] will come in."

With Dollar Shave Club, the shaving cream and aftershave they sell are natural complementary products to their gateway product, the $1 razor. The other bathroom products Dollar Shave Club sells are also, for the most part, complementary products (although some are more direct, like shaving cream, and some less direct, like One Wipe Charlies or the lip balm they sell).

For Dollar Shave Club, their supplementary products are the premium razors they offer, where I chose the mid-tier $5 razor when I first joined as a customer. The gateway product was still the main focus. After I purchased that gateway product, I was then presented with a selection of optional, supplementary products.

Similarly, you can (and should) offer both complementary and supplementary products in your business for your customers.

In the women's clothing boutique example, remember the gateway product was a comfortable, classy pair of shoes that would look great with any outfit for everyday wear. Well, what if you offered complementary products of simple, elegant socks? Or perhaps nail polish (depending on the shoe style, of course).

In the supplementary category, you could offer a more professional or high-end version for customers who prefer to dress to the nines every day. You could also provide various color or styling options, but don't get too carried away (remember, you want the gateway product decision to be simple).

Claim your **FREE business assessment**
($100 value) and unlock additional resources at
YourThriveScore.com

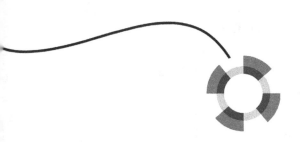

Chapter 7:

Above and Beyond

The Simple Solution to a Street Sales Team for Your Business

Once you have a customer, your relationship has only begun.

Research shows that existing customers are far more profitable than new customers.[71] If you can offer a strategic sales sequence that allows customers the opportunity to buy more (and more often) in exchange for greater transformation, you'll truly begin to generate wealth.

Some businesses have raving fans, or superfans, who will spend money to buy products and services from a given company and then brag about it and encourage their friends to do the same!

It's like a reverse-marketing expense, where customers pay you for products so they can advertise them for you, free of charge. How lucky are those business owners, right?

Wrong! Luck has nothing to do with it. You can create your own grateful, excited customers by exceeding expectations on a regular basis.

Think of it like a math equation, where a given customer's satisfaction is determined by this formula:

$$Experience - Expectation = Satisfaction$$

EXPERIENCE

EXPECTATION

If a customer walks into your business and expects a 7 or 8, and you deliver a 9, you have a positive score! That means a satisfied customer, potentially even an excited customer (you've planted the seed for a superfan).

If the same customer expects a 7 or 8, and you deliver a 5, you have a negative score. That means a dissatisfied customer, potentially even a disgruntled customer, or maybe you've lost the customer completely!

If a customer expects a 7 or 8, and you deliver a 7 or an 8, that means your score is 0. You have a neutral customer because you lived up to their expectations and did your job. You got paid, your customer is satisfied, but you won't win any awards.

Of course, the score is just a creative way to think about your customer's experience; there is no reliable way to capture your customer's expectation with a score-like number or calculate the value of the experience you provide.

For every customer, that experience is a bit different. It's subjective, as is the level of expectation when someone walks in the door.

As a side note from personal experience, this is the same rationale that you should never start a joke by telling someone you are about to share the "funniest joke ever." At this point, you have set the expectation score so high that your only hope is to live up to the experience and get out neutral, rather than ahead.

Similarly, in business, your first job is to *meet* customer expectations—but if you want to create lifelong customers and raving superfans, you are going to need to *exceed* expectations on a regular basis.

As an entrepreneur, your job is to solve a problem for a profit. Once you're clear on the real people you're serving, the real problem they're experiencing, and your real solution, you're off to the races!

By this point, you even have a measurable marketing model and a clear landscape of the various products your business offers. So, what's next? The answer's *remarkable*.

No literally, the answer to "What's next?" is that your business needs to become remarkable.

Merriam-Webster defines remarkable[72] as "worthy of being or likely to be noticed especially as being uncommon or extraordinary," but I learned what remarkable means in the South, where we like to keep it simple.

As an impressionable teenager working for Chick-fil-A, I remember my manager splitting the word into "remark" and "able" to explain that our goal was to provide such exceptional service that customers would remark on the experience to their friends and family.

For Chick-fil-A, remarkable service isn't just a pithy buzzword; it's a way of life. And it's paid off! Chick-fil-A has amassed a loyal, loving customer base that has helped them become the most profitable quick service restaurant per location and the third largest restaurant chain in the U.S., behind only McDonald's and Starbucks in total annual revenue.

In fact, they have grown to more than $12 billion in annual revenue without any outside investment (to this day, Chick-fil-A is a family-owned business).[73]

So, how did they do it? Was it their fried chicken recipe, fun waffle fries, or openly Christian values? For their customer base, all of that may have helped, but no. The key to Chick-fil-A's success lies in their second mile service strategy.

Would You Like a Second Mile?

My first "real" job was when I started working at Chick-fil-A when I was fifteen. Right away, I was taught that at Chick-fil-A, we provide "second mile service," but it took me a while to really understand what that means.

The term "second mile service" comes from a quote in Christian scripture, Matthew 5:41 (NIV), where Jesus instructs his disciples "and if anyone forces you to go one mile, go with them two miles."

Now, I'd probably heard or read that verse somewhere and nodded my head because it seemed like a generally good philosophy, but I had no idea the depth of the situation until I learned through Chick-fil-A. The message has a stronger punch to it when you consider the cultural significance of the day.

At that time in history, the Roman army had occupied most of the civilized (and semi-civilized) world. As part of maintaining their occupation, Roman soldiers traveled all over the empire, sometimes walking hundreds of miles to their next assignment, carrying bags full of armor, weapons, and supplies (up to 100 pounds).

Understandably, this was tiring travel in a time before cars, trains, or airplanes, but the Roman Empire needed their soldiers to travel, so they came up with a solution to give soldiers an occasional break.

A Roman soldier could stop people and force them to carry the soldier's pack for one mile. The civilian had to stop whatever they were doing, wherever they were, and do it without protest or complaint.

This was the scene Jesus was referring to when he said, "and if anyone forces you to go one mile, go with them two miles."

The Roman Empire, a conquering kingdom of foreigners taking over the world, required you to walk one mile with up to 100 pounds of the physical reminder of your occupation on your back. Ouch! And yet… how powerful a message would that send if when the one mile was up, you kept walking, and offered to voluntarily go two?

Chick-fil-A commissioned a dramatized video of this scene where the soldier is flabbergasted and eventually tries to stop the civilian, reminding them that they are free to go.[74] For Christ's followers, this was a tangible way they could act out "love thy enemy" with a real-world relevant (at the time) example.

For Chick-fil-A, this captured their commitment to customer service, going above and beyond any expectation a customer could possibly have. That's paid off in billions, with raving fans camping out for days before each new Chick-fil-A opens, hoping to be one of the first 100 customers inside.

Customers don't just enjoy paying money to buy Chick-fil-A products, they are seemingly in love with Chick-fil-A as a company! Dozens of creative customers have published music videos about their love for Chick-fil-A, free marketing for the company with tens of millions of views. All without a dollar of ad spend or other marketing campaign from Chick-fil-A.

The Power of Above and Beyond

Chick-fil-A took second mile service to heart early on in their customer service training. As Caleb Mathis, operator of the Chick-fil-A where I live in Columbia, Tennessee, shares,

> "Regular service, you know, getting your order right, fast service, clean restaurant, all those kinds of things are just basic needs in a dining experience, whether it's quick service or dine-in, so we call that the first mile. You expect it when you go in.
>
> "Second mile is what is not expected. It's that above and beyond. And I tell you, it seemed like a foreign concept

when it was introduced, especially for a quick service, fast food kind of environment. So, what does that look like?

"Well, that's when you're sitting at your table, and someone comes by and says, 'Can I refresh your beverage?' or 'Can I carry your tray for you?' or 'Can I remove this tray for you?' And you didn't have to get up; you didn't have to change anything—it's anticipating needs.

"And the way we inspire our team to do it isn't by telling them, 'Hey, do X, Y, and Z, and that's second mile service.' Instead, I tell them, 'Hey, this is serving from the heart. We want it to be something above and beyond but make it unique for how you want to interact with that guest that day.' I think that keeps it organic. And it's been something I think has been successful for Chick-fil-A."[75]

The point isn't the specific task; it's the fact that second mile service is above and beyond what anyone could expect to receive.

So, how can you offer your audience, your customers, second mile service? What can you do for your customers that is above and beyond what they would ever expect, where you can win their loyalty and support?

Remember, you do have to get the "first mile" right, which varies industry by industry, but that's just the start. How can you wow someone today and win their love and loyalty so they come back to read your content, share your content, and purchase your products, again and again?

First Mile First: Systemize Your Solution

Before you try and exceed anyone's expectations, you need to make sure you can meet their foundational expectations on a regular basis.

That means you need a documented process, or system, in place to deliver your products and solve customers' problems exactly as you promised during a sale.

It takes months or years of consistent delivery to earn a customer's trust, but it only takes one bad experience to destroy it.

If you are delivering your product or service a different way with each customer, you are not providing the consistency and reliability they crave.

Even if you typically deliver a similar product, but you don't have a documented system or checklist for doing it, you run the risk of missing a key part of the process when you're extra busy or you're having a bad day.

Once you add staff to the mix, you exponentially increase the risk of something going "different" even if it doesn't go wrong.

By documenting your own process, you may find ways you can improve it, or other contributors may see opportunities to consistently deliver high-quality products or services with less time, cost, and effort along the way.

I used to be a systems fanatic. I used to think you needed documented processes and thick, detailed operations manuals for every aspect of the way a business operates, so it can run like a well-oiled machine.

I gave that up when I realized that a system has no inherit, intrinsic value. A system is just a tool; the only purpose it has is to help you achieve something worthwhile (for more information on what aspects of your business to prioritize at any given moment, read *Fix This Next*[76] by Mike Michalowicz).

In this case, the system you use to deliver your products is your most important system by far. A clearly defined path to delivering your product or service is the only way to consistently deliver an experience your customer is looking for, regardless of who delivers the product or when.

I should note, just because you have a clearly documented process does not guarantee you will meet customer expectations.

Of course, something could go wrong along the way, but your system (or checklist) dramatically increases your chance of success.

There will always be some customers who have such a high expectation that you cannot meet it, and the best you can hope for is to meet their high expectations with great effort and come out neutral, rather than ahead.

More than likely, you can't help those customers. You're destined to end up leaving them dissatisfied, so you might as well part ways early on.

Your Superfan Strategy

When you consistently surprise and delight your customers, and exceed their expectations, you start with happy customers. Over time, some of those customers can become superfans. As Kevin Kelly illustrated in his 1,000 True Fans essay,[77]

> "Of course, not every fan will be super. While the support of a thousand true fans may be sufficient for a living, for every single true fan, you might have two or three regular fans. Think of concentric circles with true fans at the center and a wider circle of regular fans around them. These regular fans may buy your creations occasionally or may have bought only once. But their ordinary purchases expand your total income. Perhaps they bring in an additional 50%. Still, you want to focus on the super fans because the enthusiasm of true fans can increase the patronage of regular fans. True fans not only

are the direct source of your income, but also your chief marketing force for the ordinary fans."

Perry Marshall goes further in *80/20 Sales and Marketing*,[78] where he demonstrates that 20% of your customers will pay ten times as much as the average customer if your offer is compelling enough. If you've built up enough goodwill with your customers, you can take that one step further and 20% of that 20% group of customers (4% of your total customer base) will pay ten times as much, again.

This concept has become so powerfully clear in online businesses with direct access to consumers that Pat Flynn, founder of Smart Passive Income, wrote the book *Superfans* to teach entrepreneurs how to cultivate a superfan-focused experience. As Pat shared when I interviewed him,[79]

"It's not just about getting them on your email list and having them run through some automation. Like that's helpful. And that's a part of the process. But that's not the whole story. It's not just about getting a person to become a customer. They make a sale, you make a sale, and then boom, you win and everybody's happy. No, it's the entire customer journey from when a person finds you for the first time. How to create activation moments for them to want to dive deeper into your stuff. To subscribe, to follow, to purchase something, that's step one. Step two, then, is to make them feel like they're a part of a community like what I'm doing here with the income stream every morning on YouTube or creating live streams on Facebook or an event or highlighting and spotlighting. It's like how Donald Miller talks about in StoryBrand, spotlighting the heroes within your audiences. You have them all support each other in creating moments of opportunity to then level them up to superfan status. You can create little personalized moments over time to ultimately help people feel like they belong.

"That's ultimately where we as humans want to be. We want to be with people who make us feel like we belong, who make us feel heard, who make us feel recognized, right? And so, we as creators, as facilitators, as hosts... we have the ability to do this. We've always had the ability to do this, but we've been so focused on growing our brand with SEO and paid ads and getting on all the different platforms so we can reach new people (and it's always about finding new people). I think if we just focused instead—or at least exerted maybe even half that energy on the people who are with us already—it's ultimately gonna help you grow your brand from within."

This strategy of serving above and beyond expectations works well in any industry because it turns out your customers are real people who have real lives and real personal experiences, and they appreciate when they feel special (just like you do, when you're a customer yourself).

Sean Harper, CEO of Kin Insurance, took a superfan strategy with his digital-first insurance company into the homeowners insurance industry with great success. As he shared,[80]

"A normal insurance company might have a net promoter score of 40, which is pretty good for insurance. Ours is 80. Wow. So, we just take much better care of our customers than has-been legacy insurance companies do, and we try to treat them like family. That's our name, and we take that seriously."

What would that be like, for you, if your customers experienced "second mile service" in a way that led them to tell everyone they could about how much they love your business? How can you love on your customers in every interaction with your business from here on out?

Relationships > Results

I have this phrase written in my notebook, and I'll often rewrite it on my whiteboard or the corner of my desk: Relationships > Results.

It has a double meaning because the symbol in the middle means "greater than" to remind me that relationships are greater than, and more important than, results. The double meaning shows up when you look back at that symbol as an arrow and realize that relationships lead to results.

Both are true! That's the win-win reality of betting on relationships first. When you prioritize relationships, the results will follow. They always do.

In your business, that includes the relationships with your employees and partners, but for the purpose of this book, our focus is the relationship you have with your customers, and potential customers, in your business.

This entire marketing and sales framework stems from that one decision about your target customer because you can't have a relationship until you know which real people you are setting out to develop a relationship with.

Once you do know your target customer, you can grow to understand them and test your ability to understand them by offering valuable assistance in the form of your products and services, designed to serve.

That's why empathy is such a critical skill to develop in business. Your business depends on your ability to understand another person's perspective. The empathy advantage sets your business apart from self-centered companies that exist to sell products, maximize shareholder value, or simply "to grow."

Once you orient your business toward service, you unlock a supercharged sales process that is enjoyable to operate because you're a healthy human, and healthy humans enjoy helping other humans! We're designed to work together, not just during our downtime but also during business hours (perhaps even more so, then).

Relationships are more important than results, and relationships lead to results. Relationships > Results! As Pat Flynn expounded when I interviewed him about *Superfans*,[81]

> "This is business insurance. My opinion is platform agnostic; it doesn't matter what happens with technology, your fans will follow you; they become the lifeblood of your business. These are the repeat customers; these are the people who are going to show up for you when you are in dire need. They're going to be there to defend you from trolls on the frontlines before you even know they exist. And they're going to be with you, like I mentioned earlier, to give you honest feedback when you don't know what to do next, because they are your target audience."

*Claim your **FREE business assessment** ($100 value) and unlock additional resources at YourThriveScore.com*

Chapter 8:

Predict, Don't Prophesy

Make Financial Decisions Based on Reality, Not Hope

I was so confused the first time I started using the personal budgeting app YNAB (You Need A Budget). There was nowhere to enter how much money I expected to make this month, and when I started listing expected expenses, YNAB quickly flagged me as over budget, in the red!

I poked around a bit before I discovered that this was entirely by design because YNAB helps you budget based on money you actually have in your bank account, right now. Not money you plan to have, or money you expect to have in the future, but money that you actually have. Jesse Mecham, the founder of

YNAB, refers to this as a core rule in his financial framework, "Age Your Money."[82] As their website explains,

> "You aren't stressed because you're not living on the financial edge. No more wasting time and energy timing bills to a specific paycheck. When a bill comes, you just pay it. The result? Breathing room. Less focus on today and more on tomorrow means bigger thinking, better decisions, and chiseled abs (it's possible!)."

That approach is a bit unusual, but it's actually very simple, and it makes sense. It might explain why YNAB is much more than a simple piece of software; they have amassed a loyal following of thousands of customers who credit YNAB with their financial freedom and peace of mind (just check out YouNeedaBudget.com/blog).

I realized that up until I started using YNAB myself, I was playing prophet with my financial future, creating a budget based on the money I planned or hoped to earn each month. The truth is that until money is actually in your bank account, it's not yours. The same is true in your business. Are you making financial decisions based on reality or on hope?

In your business or personal life, what would you do if an unexpected major expense came up, a payment was late, or there was simply a glitch in the bank transfer system? Would you be able to adjust your expenses comparatively or would you have already committed to spending based on the money you expected to take in?

Josh Fonger, an entrepreneur and business consultant from Work the System, put it this way in an interview about his business during the Great Reset,[83]

"I've got a business mentor, and we were talking a few months back, and I told him I had these plans for this year, and I had all these things I was going to do. And I'll be giving strategic advice to a lot of clients. And he said, Josh, when did you know the future? Like, was there a time in your life when you did know the future? So, just to kind of put it into perspective in terms of what we actually have control over and what we don't, and we can obviously make estimates, we should make plans to set goals. But, whenever we presuppose, these black swan events are going to happen. We're kidding ourselves, right? We're going beyond our own intellectual capacity. And it's better to stick with what we do have control over like, what am I going to do during this hour? What am I going to do during the next hour? What am I going to do with my team during the meeting? Now, what are we doing right here, right now, and be hyperfocused on making wins and having success with each moment. So, that gave me some real perspective."

Most business owners make financial decisions based on their goals, hiring or expanding based on what they expect to generate in revenue this quarter or year. In good times, that doesn't seem like a problem. It's exhilarating to map out a product launch, generate six- or seven-figures in revenue, and then do a little happy dance as you watch the dollars accumulate in your bank account! But it's risky.

In good times, it feels safe, but in bad times (or simply a seasonal downturn) spending based on projections is dangerous. Even in good times, sometimes product launches simply go wrong. It's depressing to spend tens of thousands of dollars on a product launch that bombs and makes almost no money but leaves you footing the promotional bill.

The key to building a profitable business in any economy is running a business that has both adaptability and predictability built in. If you make financial decisions based on real results after they happen, you have a built-in runway to adapt as your results change. If something changes in your market, or an economic crisis sneaks up on you, you'll have room to adapt.

Running businesses based on financial prophecy was always a bit dangerous, but this became devastating when the Great Reset hit. Many businesses had already spent or committed huge expenses based on expected revenue and were left hanging onto a negative ledger after just a couple of weeks.

After just a few weeks of economic downturn, 32% of small business owners started missing loan payments.[84] Major corporations like Panera Bread, Victoria's Secret, and Barnes & Noble simply stopped paying rent.[85]

As Warren Buffett refers to moments like these, "You only find out who is swimming naked when the tide goes out."[86] Nobody likes feeling vulnerable, and exposed, so it's time we all took stock and asked ourselves how we make financial decisions. Are you spending money based on what you hope to earn or based on what you already have?

What about Spending Money to Make Money?

Depending on your background, you may be scratching your head at the idea of waiting to spend money until you've already earned enough revenue to offset the expenses. Perhaps you've heard that "you need to spend money to make money" or something similar, but that's not really true.

Sure, when you are just starting out it's helpful to have an initial influx of money from investors, your bank, or yourself, but with most business models, this is a one-time investment before your business revenues kick in and should fund your continued operations and growth. As well, with today's abundance of platforms, your up-front investment can be very little; some business models require no up-front investment at all, other than your personal time.

Even if your business relies on paid promotion to operate, you should build a cash flow buffer in your business so that you are not paying for advertisements out of the current month's revenue (more on that in chapter 10). Similarly, you can budget for future promotions with a preset percentage of each month's revenue (more on that coming up in chapter 9).

This approach of using existing resources to finance operations and growth is broadly referred to as "bootstrapping" and is dismissed by many venture capitalist investors as a cop-out, in direct contrast to the standard Silicon Valley approach of "go big or go home."

The bootstrap approach flies in the face of a culture that elevates high-growth companies, whether based on venture capital funding or self-funded marketing campaigns. To fund yourself in any economy, you may need to consciously commit to slow your growth—but probably less than you think.

What Is a High-Growing Company Worth to You?

Some people argue that bootstrapping a business limits how fast you can grow, and maybe that's true. Rather than dispute that, I'd rather ask why you want to grow your business at all? Growth, for the sake of growth, has no inherent value. Growing your business is wonderful—when you're growing sustainably and enjoying the work along the way.

Every year, *Inc.* magazine publishes the Inc. 5000 list of the fastest-growing privately held companies in America, and it's a prestigious award to be included in. I've worked with several different companies that have hit the Inc. 5000 list, and there is an adrenaline rush that comes from seeing your business on the list (and seeing where you rank on the list, once you make it). I've also worked with companies that hit the list multiple times, which is an extra dose of fun.

But the Inc. 5000, and similar lists like it, have a big problem. They base success on year-over-year topline revenue growth, which can hide problems beneath the surface of the company reports, inside the organization itself. The Kauffman Foundation partnered with *Inc.* to follow up on past award winners and discovered that roughly two-thirds ended up failing within a few years.[87]

Growth is not all it's cracked up to be. Some companies that hit the Inc. 5000 list are phenomenal, based on a foundational culture and long-term business model beyond their immediate revenue growth—but I personally know entrepreneurs who have burned through staff, broken up with business partners, or gone through a divorce in their personal life while hitting the Inc. 5000 at the same time.

Growth, by itself, is neutral. It's neither inherently good nor inherently bad, so why do you want to grow your business? What level of growth are you after, and why? If you accomplish your goals, and are satisfied, what will that make possible in your business or personal life?

In some industries, people will tell you that growth is a requirement because of the need to amass "market share" and "dominate," but I don't buy that. It's an outdated concept based on a supply-based economy rather than today's attention economy.

The attention economy is not about hoarding demand; it's about getting people's attention—and while some people treat demand much like supply, it's not the same. Consumers can and do purchase products from many different companies to solve a similar need.

Think about it, how many people or businesses do you pay attention to that sell similar products? Do you shop on Amazon. com as well as a local bookstore? Do you buy coffee at Starbucks sometimes, and also buy beans and equipment elsewhere to make your own coffee at home? There are ways to solve similar problems with similar solutions, no monopoly required.

A Look at How Seasonal Businesses Manage Fluctuations

In the middle of 2020, during the Great Reset, I interviewed entrepreneurs about how they were adapting, as part of the Survive and Thrive podcast.

One of the entrepreneurs I interviewed, Josh Fonger, shared some great insight on how the fundamentals of surviving and thriving in crisis are a way of life for highly seasonal businesses, like landscaping or tax preparation services. As Josh said,[88]

> "I'm not too concerned about dips and cash flow. I work with seasonal businesses, and they have pretty dramatic dips and cash flow for six months every year. And they're fine. Right? So, the business fundamentals, I don't tie to the last two month's cash flow because I don't think that's a good representation. I think you can really lose perspective if you live in that world. And what we do with

seasonal businesses is you have to cut the bleeding, and the biggest bleeding for those kinds of businesses that are brick-and-mortar are typically payroll, and so you have to cut that. You can't just be a nice person and then just eat that for three months. It doesn't work, right? They're going to come back to a business that doesn't exist."

Businesses that recognize they are seasonal, with periodic spikes in revenue with lulls in between, survive and thrive because they manage their finances well and pay close attention to when demand changes throughout the year. They may expand or shrink their staff and other expenses based on seasonal changes to their business, regularly trimming the fat to ensure a seasonal spike in revenue supports the business all year round.

The reality is on some level all businesses are "seasonal" businesses because none of us are immune to the fluctuations of socioeconomic conditions in our global hyperconnected world. The approach that seasonal businesses take to conserve spending is one we can all learn from and apply to any industry as a savvy entrepreneurial approach.

How to Set Reasonable-Yet-Risky Goals

Moving forward, you need a new framework for setting goals with your team. If you are making financial decisions based on the funds you currently have, it can be tempting to set lower than usual goals. That would be a mistake.

For the last three years, I've worked closely with Michael Hyatt and his team. Michael is a bestselling author and highly successful CEO, but he is also widely known for his productivity and goal-setting philosophy, taught in his training, built into the Full Focus

Planner, and detailed in his #1 *Wall Street Journal* bestseller *Your Best Year Ever.*

One of the most counterintuitive insights that Michael shares is how effective goals need to be risky. In fact, goal theorists Edwin A. Locke and Gary P. Latham compiled the results from 400 different studies and concluded,

> "There is a linear relationship between the degree of goal difficulty and performance… The performance of participants with the highest goals was over 250% higher than those with the easiest goals."[89]

As Michael explains, "We rise to a challenge, but we lay back when it's easy." Goals need to make sense for the stage of your business or personal life, but they also need to be in your "discomfort zone" enough that your goals will challenge you to grow.[90]

I find this to be true, that risky goals inspire creative thinking and goals that are too comfortable or too easy tend to lead to making minimal progress by maintaining the status quo. Then again, risky goals can inspire risky behavior, can't they?

People are motivated by exciting, risky goals. So, how do you balance prudence and ambition? How do you balance the need to make wise financial decisions while also reaching beyond your comfort zone? Raymond Aaron is glad you asked. Here's what he has to say about goal setting:

> "I call the bad way to write a goal the Dreaded Binary Technique. It looks like this: 'I will be the top salesman in the company this month.' What's wrong with this goal? I'm sure it is exactly how you would write such a goal.

Indeed, it is the way 100% of all goal-writers write their goals. What's wrong is that it is binary—you achieve it or you don't achieve it. If you achieve it, you feel good. If you don't achieve it, you feel bad. Why would you want to set up a system that gives you some reasonable probability of failure and feeling bad? The reason is that you don't know any other technique."[91]

When I interviewed Raymond about the problem with traditional goal setting, he added this anecdote,

"If I asked you at the end of a month, how was your month? You'd say, 'I guess it was okay. Kind of good.' You'd say kind of weak English words."[92]

Raymond goes on to introduce his "MTO Technique" (which I use myself). As Raymond explains,

"MTO stands for Minimum, Target, Outrageous. If you intend on setting a goal like you want to run a 10K, let's say, and you want to run a 10K in an hour, and there is a 10K race during this month… If you say, 'I'm going to run a 10K in an hour,' you have a binary result. Either you run it in an hour and you say 'Yay,' or you don't run it (or don't run it in an hour) and you say, 'boo, I did bad.' And since you only write goals in which you're bad in, you have a high chance of not achieving it.

"Let me give you an example. You would never write a goal like 'I am going to brush my teeth every morning and every night this whole month.' You already do it. Right? But you would write a goal that 'I'm going to meditate every morning. I'm going to jog every morning. I'm going to stretch every morning.' You'd only write goals on what you're not good at. Well, if you write goals on what you're not good at, you have a high chance of not achieving it. And if you fail consistently, you'll pretty soon stop doing it. So MTO relieves you of that horror because you don't write goals in the dreaded binary way of maybe you'll get it, maybe you don't get it; you triumvirate your goals; you triage your goals. Outrageous is what you know you cannot achieve."[93]

Instead of setting a single success target for each goal, you break every goal into three levels:

1. Minimum: What you can count on, based on actual past performance
2. Target: A stretch beyond what you know you can accomplish
3. Outrageous: What you know you cannot achieve

When you set MTO goals, you create three levels of achievement you can accomplish with each goal, and you dramatically increase your chance of succeeding. This is a balanced approach of both reasonable and risky.

Raymond describes the results of an MTO sales goal like this,[94]

"You will most likely achieve your Minimum, since that is what you typically do. Maybe you attain seven sales by the twenty-second day of the month. You then look at your goal and realize that you've only got two sales to go to hit your Target. That will inspire you to go for it. If you achieve your Target, then you are even happier; nevertheless, even if you hit only seven or eight, you have still achieved your goal (at least to the Minimum), and you feel great. If you actually achieve Target, you are elated. And the increased self-esteem you generate each month will soon propel you up into the Outrageous category."

Why set an Outrageous goal that you know you cannot achieve? Well, as Raymond explains:

> "Just because you think you can't achieve it doesn't mean you're not going to achieve it. Just because you write it down, your mind starts creating it in ways you could never even believe—coincidence of bumping into people or seeing an app that can dramatically improve your performance or something."

The MTO Technique Applied to Financial Goals

I have been using MTO goals in my own business ventures for the last five years with great success. I find this goal framework works for financial planning best of all. Here's how it works:

Set your Minimum goal based on a safe projection of revenue based on past performance, either by product launch or quarter or fiscal year. This becomes the base threshold you need to break even or continue to meet your financial commitments (either for a specific product or the business as a whole, this works either way). This should be the number built into your budget.

The Target goal is what you want to hit. Depending on your industry, this might be 10%–100% higher than the Minimum goal. This is what your strategy is built around and any rewards you've set for yourself or your team. This should be in your discomfort zone but still well within reach.

The Outrageous goal is where things really get fun. This is, like the name says, a goal that is outrageous because it is so large and so far above your Target goal that it is impossible (but impossible things happen every day). I love to set Outrageous goals at least 50% higher than a Target goal, but I've set them to double the Target as well.

These are important because sometimes a project works better than you expect, and you hit your Target goal right away! When that happens, you want to already have your Outrageous goal set so you can ride that wave and set your sights on the impossible (and you just might hit it).

Don't expect to hit your Outrageous goal often, but when you do, your entire team will walk around like reigning champions for weeks. It is an exciting, contagious energy! Even when you fall short of your Outrageous goal, anything over your Target goal is an absolute win and worth celebrating too.

In fact, because you base financial expenditures on past behavior—and that's also what determines your Minimum goal—the difference between your Minimum and Target should be almost pure profit, other than your Cost of Goods Sold.

For example, let's say you own a coffee shop and you want to set monthly financial goals for your business that you can share with your team. Looking at the last six months of sales, you see that the average monthly revenue is $12,500, but you're also currently growing 15% year-over-year. The coming month is September, and the last few years you've seen your revenue drop 10% in September as the school year begins.

With this information in hand, your MTO goals might look like this:

- Minimum: $11,250
- Target: $12,500
- Outrageous: $15,000

The Minimum goal here is based on six months of average monthly revenue, with the seasonal percentage of September baked in. In other words, this is what you can count on based on actual past performance. Another way to set this goal would have been simply to copy and paste September's monthly revenue from the previous year.

The Target goal here is a stretch, but not a huge one. In this case, hitting $12,500 would require some creative marketing or sales strategies to make up the seasonal gap typically seen in September and maintain the recent monthly average (which, remember, is actually 15% year-over-year growth).

The Outrageous goal here is within the realm of possibility, right? It's not impossible, but it is well beyond any past performance and would represent a much higher growth rate than the 15% year-over-year growth rate experienced so far.

The point here is not the specific numbers in this example. Your business may have a few extra zeros on the end of those goals, but the point is that the MTO Technique allows you to balance risk and reality to motivate yourself and your team while also building a predictable financial strategy at the core of your business.

How Do You Make Financial Decisions?

Crisis or no crisis, most businesses fail within the first five years.[95] Many business owners chalk that failure up to not enough customers, but they usually mean "not enough customers paying enough money to cover all of our expenses plus enough profit to make it worth my while."

The point here is that you do want to set goals that excite yourself and your team, and you want to pursue them with enthusiasm—but you don't want to budget or make financial decisions based on your Target or Outrageous goals until you've already hit them and the money is sitting in your bank. Until then, goals are just that: goals. There is no guarantee of your success (so don't act like it by spending as if you already won).

Predictable finances are important, especially when it comes to how you calculate what you're willing to spend at any given time. That's why this is a foundational question in the ThriveScore assessment—but even this is not binary, there are several approaches that will help your overall sustainability (and thus, your score).

Claim your **FREE business assessment** *($100 value) and unlock additional resources at YourThriveScore.com*

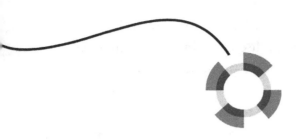

Chapter 9:

Prioritize Profit First

The Only Consistent Cure Is Cold, Hard Cash

While there are many ways to grow revenue and keep expenses in check to grow profit, I prefer the simplest route. Rather than rely on willpower, a daily math exercise, and guesswork, I find it more helpful to implement a systematic approach to generating profit. One that has built-in checks and balances to act as gutter guards so you're more likely to strike out!

A Brief Introduction to Profit First

Most people think of profit as Sales – Expenses = Profit, or the more financially literate might use Gross Income – Gross Expenses = Net Income and then land on a profit number from there. Both equations are textbook correct—but practically useless.

Most profit calculations are rear-facing metrics, so by the time you've calculated your profit, all you have are the leftovers, and the rest is already spent. This last insight was inspired by Mike Michalowicz in his book *Profit First: Transform Your Business from a Cash-Eating Monster to a Money-Making Machine.* As the title implies, rather than thinking of profit as the money that's leftover, why not calculate profit first?

Mike's system, Profit First, is articulated in his blog and bestselling book, but also by a fleet of certified Profit First Professionals who practice Profit First accounting with countless business clients across the globe. Profit First has helped many entrepreneurs rethink their business relationship with money, and simultaneously left some accountants shaking their heads that the system is "unnecessary" as they point to a stack of financial reports.

It's true, you can get all the financial information you need to make calculated business decisions from reading your cash flow and profit & loss statements in your accounting software—but will you? And will your bookkeeping always be caught up to the current day?

Mike Michalowicz brilliantly describes the accounting method most entrepreneurs practice as "Bank Balance Accounting"

"You look at your bank balance and see a chunk of change. Yippee! You feel great for about ten minutes, and then decide to pay all the bills that have been piling up.

The balance goes to zero, and very quickly, you feel that all-too-familiar tightening in the chest…

"I'm going to go out on a limb and guess that you only look at your income statement on occasion. I suspect you rarely look at your cash flow statements or balance sheet. And if you do, I doubt you review these docs on a daily basis or understand exactly what they say. But I bet you check your bank account every day, don't you? It's OK. If you look at your bank account daily, I want to congratulate you because that means you are a typical— scratch that—a normal business leader; that's how most entrepreneurs behave."[96]

Most financial systems simply track and project where you have already earned and spent money, and the more advanced include where you think you will earn and spend in the near future.

Profit First, instead, puts hard boundaries on the flow of your finances. It starts with flipping the traditional accounting formula on its head so that expenses are based on what's leftover and profit always comes first:

> ### Sales – Profit = Expenses

Practically, that means that as money flows into your business, you split it into dedicated bank accounts for different purposes. That way, at a glance, you have a complete view of where your money is and where you can spend it (along with where you cannot).

According to basic algebra, "Sales – Profit = Expenses" and "Sales – Expenses = Profit" are equal, but practically speaking, they are completely different. This is because of Parkinson's Law, which states, "Work expands so as to fill the time available for its completion."[97]

I'm sure you've experienced Parkinson's Law yourself, where you have two hours left in your workday to tackle an important project, and it takes the full two hours. Then the following week, you have a similar project but this time you have the full day available, so the project takes you the full day to complete!

The point of Profit First is to use Parkinson's Law to your advantage and limit the operating expenses your business can take on in order to guarantee you generate profit (and get paid) month after month.

Why Profit First Is Important

You need your financial system to help you drive your business the way you drive your car: 90% of your visibility is forward so you can see where you're going through a large, clear windshield. Looking back, all you need is a small rearview mirror to stay on track.

Profit First is more than just a bunch of bank accounts; it's a system with a built-in philosophy of financial business decisions that mean you spend no more than you earn, you always pay yourself, and you stay out of debt.

This means you're building a cash flow positive business (more on that in chapter 10), which is truly a system that generates wealth. This also means that you are bootstrapping your company by setting aside a small percentage of each customer payment to fund your growing operations.

When I interviewed Mike Michalowicz, he gave special emphasis to the importance of setting tax dollars aside, in a separate bank account from the rest of your business,

"The biggest bill associated with the operation of a business that we're least prepared for is our tax bill. It's a massive bill. That's guaranteed that the more money you make, the more the government's going to take. And we've got to be prepared for it. So, I have a tax account whereas my business generates revenue, a percentage of that goes into a tax account as reserved. And listen, the government plays no games. It will punch you in the face. If you don't pay, it will come after you hard."[98]

Many business owners rely on quarterly estimates or annual reports from their accountant to tell them how much money they owe in taxes, but that tax liability is created the minute the revenue comes into your business. So, if you're not setting taxes aside proactively, your bank account is giving you a distorted view of your available financial resources at any given time.

Practicing Percentage-Based Budgets

I'm sorry to say it, but dollar-based budgets are laughably impractical in business, as long as you intend to remain flexible and lean into (or out of) profitable opportunities as they arise.

You're probably familiar with the process. I've been a part of it countless times, and even made seven-figure dollar-based budgets myself! You get in a room with a whiteboard and a spreadsheet, map out every project you plan to tackle in the next quarter or year, and then do some rough math to estimate how much each project will cost and how much you will earn.

Once everyone at the table is satisfied that your budget is plausible, everyone leaves the room and you create bonus plans, hiring plans, and marketing plans based off of the educated guess you collectively made as a group. I'll give you bonus points if you made the budget based on historical financial data or demographic research, but most companies don't even do that.

Dollar-based budgets work much like a brand-new car. They immediately start to lose value as soon as you leave the room or drive off the lot. The real world leaves a mark, and the shiny new budget loses its new car smell right away.

That's why percentage-based budgets are so powerful. They provide boundaries that keep spending in check, but they also help companies remain nimble by building in a framework for scaling spending up or down based on actual sales, real revenue results.

Think about it, what if you knew that 30% of Net Income in your business was set aside for operations costs? Within those operations costs, you could divide the budget further into overhead and marketing, along with any other important categories, but the bigger picture of 30% of Net Income set aside for operations would immediately set clear boundaries on your spending.

If you generate $10,000 in Net Income, then you can set aside $3,000 for operations. If you generate $50,000 in Net Income, then you can set aside $15,000 for operations instead. You don't need to spend the full budget all at once, but you can watch that budget grow (or shrink) to match your actual income and then choose where to strategically invest your operations expense.

That's the power of percentage-based budgets; they scale up and down as needed based on how your business is performing, rather than how much you think you should spend. Profit First is a percentage-based budgeting system, but what categories should you create, and how much should you set aside for each category? Mike Michalowicz is glad you asked.

Set Target Allocation Percentages

The first edition of Profit First was published in 2014 after Mike had already seen firsthand how his system could help business owners thrive, and thousands of business owners in different industries have adopted the financial system since then, on their own or working directly with Mike Michalowicz and his team of Profit First Professionals.

That's allowed Mike to get an inside view into businesses of all shapes and sizes and create a benchmark for your "Target Allocation Percentages," or the percentages you should set aside for each key category in your business.

The biggest variable from one business model to another, on a financial statement, is the Cost of Goods Sold. In other words, how much revenue from each sale goes directly to covering the cost of delivering that product or service? Subtract that from your total revenue and you get Net Income—what Profit First considers "Real Revenue," which is where your percentage-based budget kicks in.

In Profit First, these are considered your "Target Allocation Percentages" and in the most basic implementation of this system, you should have four categories (though in more advanced versions of Profit First, you may have as many as ten).[99]

For example, in a small business making less than $500,000 per year in "Real Revenue," the benchmark Profit First Target Allocation Percentages would be:

- 5% Profit
- 50% Owner's Pay
- 30% Operations
- 15% Taxes

These benchmarks are only a guideline for getting started so you have something to compare to and work toward (even if you start with a 1% profit allocation instead). At each level of revenue, your business needs will be different, and more than likely the percentage you set aside for owner's pay will decrease over time— even as the real dollars paid to you increase.

Admittedly, Operations is a broad category and you may want to break that down further (personally I prefer a dedicated marketing and advertising allocation). You may want a specific allocation for payroll, or another industry-specific investment. The point is to clarify your percentage-based budget guidelines by deciding on your Target Allocation Percentages to start.

Open Separate Bank Accounts

Setting a percentage-based budget is helpful, but it can be hard to keep up with when you're running your business from day to day. That's why Mike Michalowicz recommends physically separating your allocation categories by opening multiple checking and savings accounts.

To practice Profit First, Mike recommends turning your primary checking account for your business into an Income account. This is the bank account where all transaction payments should come in, whether they come from online transactions, invoices, or your cash register.

Then, twice a month you should transfer the accumulated income from that account to at least four separate bank accounts for your business, based on those predetermined percentage rates:

- Owner's Pay (Checking). This is the bank account where you accumulate income you set aside to pay yourself. No matter your legal structure, you can average out your income to pay yourself a paycheck from this account with a simple biweekly transfer.

- Profit (Savings). This is exactly what it sounds like; you set aside a percentage of all income as profit first, before expenses, and only withdraw funds from here once each business quarter as a profit payout—write yourself a profit check, then cash it!
- Operations (Checking). This is the bank account where you set aside funds to pay for fixed and variable expenses to run your business, from marketing to accounting and everything in between.
- Tax (Savings). This is essentially your prepayment account to set aside funds for tax payments. Use this to pay local, state, or federal taxes as needed without any surprise bills.

If you have employees, you should create an additional payroll account, and depending on the timing and size of your production costs, you may want an account for that purpose as well.

You would be surprised how simple it is to set this up. Really. It sounds complicated, but once you talk to your bank or local credit union, you should have no trouble opening multiple accounts. It's a financial management system that keeps your money in the right place at the right time and controls spending so you see more profit and owner's pay income each month.

It also means that at any point in time you can glance at your bank account dashboard to get a snapshot of your financial situation and your resources in each area of your business. You avoid the risk of inadvertently including your tax liability or your protected payroll in the total available cash for an operations investment or marketing pivot that you want to make.

Scott Beebe, from Business On Purpose, put it a bit more directly when I interviewed him,

> "It's like this pill, this rope to save you from the cliff. And if you don't do it, you're just going to jump off. Trying to run your business from one or two bank accounts is just insanity."[100]

Implementing Profit First isn't just a good financial decision, it's a good emotional decision as well. Scott has spent years coaching hundreds of small business owners, and he tells a familiar story of the hard side of the entrepreneur life that many small business owners experience,

> "We just had a business owner here locally this week who told one of our coaches, 'I wake up at 2 a.m. every morning' just because he's stressed, like he's got all this stuff swimming in his head. He said, 'I just can't sleep. And then I go back for another fitful hour or two, and then wake up and do it all over again.' This guy's thirty, young family, you know, running a nice-sized business in town, and everybody drives by his businesses like 'Oh, my gosh, he's killing it. He's killing it!' And the reality is, the business is kind of killing him."

Profit First doesn't solve all your business problems, but it does remove a massive amount of guesswork and stress so you can sleep well at night and enjoy the fruits of your labor, the long-term wealth that builds up over time.

I remember the first business quarter I started using Profit First, back in 2016. I started small, but a few months later, I got my first quarterly profit check (from myself) in the mail for $500! I seriously considered sending that check to Mike Michalowicz to thank him for Profit First, but unfortunately for him (and fortunately for me), I took my wife on a celebratory weekend getaway instead.

I had a chance to share that with Mike, and his response surprised me,

> "That's the goal, because when you rewarded yourself and your wife, it started building the muscle and you want to repeat it. And honestly, you spent money, which means you contributed to our economy, which means you bolstered it. So, you are serving me. You're serving everyone. So, well done, John!"[101]

Mike said it best. There is nothing selfish about paying yourself for your hard work. On the contrary, making more profit is a way to serve everyone! So even if you need to start small and make a tiny profit allocation at first, that's symbolic of your long-term commitment to building a profitable business that generates wealth for yourself, your family, and the world.

How Often Does Your Business Generate Profit?

How you generate profit is ultimately less important than the fact that you do generate profit consistently in your business. Profit First is a breakthrough financial system for maximizing the profit you do generate through your business, but there are other systems you can use, and many profitable businesses use traditional accounting rather than Profit First.

Regardless, profitability is foundational to the sustainability of your business venture. That is why it's a key ingredient of your ThriveScore. Have you taken your free assessment yet, at YourThriveScore.com? Take that now, and you can measure your progress over time.

If you're not profitable, you need to get profitable ASAP. Otherwise, it's only a matter of time until you're out of business and everyone on your payroll is unemployed. This is why Profit First is so important, just like YNAB for personal budgets.

An emergency fund is also important, but your emergency fund is a static resource—Profit First helps you keep the same financial prudence in your fluid, day-to-day business. So, you may need to rebuild your budget from scratch when you look at your operations account and realize that limits what you can spend.

Start with what you have to pay, such as contractual obligations like your mortgage or rent. If even those are an issue, talk to your bank or your landlord to negotiate an adjustment of some kind.

Your landlord is an entrepreneur also, so you can't expect them to offer free rent, but they may be willing to agree to a deferral where you get a few months without rent to pivot and then your rent begins at an adjusted, higher rate (I was able to negotiate a similar agreement with the landlord over my coworking space when COVID-19 forced us to temporarily close just fifty-eight days after our grand opening).

Once you have a plan to cover your contractual overhead, you need to make sure you can cover supplies for what you have to sell, your Cost of Goods in terms of inventory, raw suppliers, or production costs. Without products or services to sell, you're out of business so that must come first. Only then can you pay for sales and support staff, because they are important, but they won't be able to work without products to sell!

After all those needs are met, if you have anything left, you can invest in your other operational expenses including marketing cost. If you are new to Profit First, you may need to ease into it with a meager percentage set aside for profit or owner's pay, and that's okay as long as you improve that allocation over time.

> ### Claim your **FREE business assessment**
> *($100 value) and unlock additional resources at*
> *YourThriveScore.com*

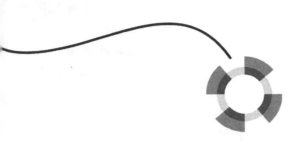

Chapter 10:

Charge Up Front

Design a Business, Not a Bank (Unless You're a Bank)

n case you're not familiar with the term, in layman's terms "cash flow" is simply the amount of money (cash) moving in and out of your business at any given time, representing the fluid nature of income and expenses from day to day in any business.

Cash flow insolvency happened before the Great Reset, but it is all the more real in the midst of a landscape where many businesses can't open their doors to sell inventory they have, so their "assets" prove useless at the end of the day. Despite that, I've heard small business owners refer to their inventory as a safety net. Saying things like "Yeah, so we have investments just laying around. It's all these assets we can liquidate if we need to."

Situations like this were unfortunately common during the Great Recession of 2008, where companies like Chrysler and General Motors filed bankruptcy and relied on government bailouts to recover, even though they had tens of billions of dollars in assets in their possession. When Lehman Brothers filed bankruptcy, they had nearly $700 billion in assets.[102]

Michael Hyatt, who was the CEO of Thomas Nelson publishers at the time, watched Lehman Brothers declare bankruptcy from a Wells Fargo office in Manhattan, where he had a full day of meetings with investors (who all canceled as they scrambled to adapt). That crisis shaped his approach to business, as he recognized the importance of cash flow management. As he shared,

> "During the Great Recession, we got very aggressive about our cash management. That was the first time as a leader that I ever started having weekly cash flow meetings where we were projecting the next 16 weeks of cash, what our receipts were going to be, and what our disbursements were going to be. And if we're going to be in trouble through every one of those periods. So, one of the things we've done ever since I started Michael Hyatt & Company was a cash flow meeting where I get together with what I call our Executive Committee, but it's our CFO and my COO. And we meet once a week—we still do that to this day—and we look at the next 16 weeks, week by week, what our cash receipts, our cash disbursements, and our cash balances are going to be week by week."[103]

It is important to understand the true lifeblood of a business is not found in the Profit & Loss statements or quarterly earnings reports; it's found in bank accounts. As Michael Hyatt put it, "your ability to continue to generate cash is everything. I mean, it's like oxygen to a diver. It will determine how long you can stay down, or in this case, how long you can stay in business. If you run out of cash, you're done."[104]

Becoming Cash Flow Positive Is Your Choice to Make

Many business owners recognize the importance of cash, but most fail to understand that cash flow is predominantly a symptom of business design. In other words, whether or not your business is cash flow positive is up to you. Allan Dib described this well,

> "Probably 70% of your success is choosing the right business model because you can be an amazing entrepreneur but just in the wrong business model. And that's going to be the difference between you doing mediocre financially versus you doing very, very well financially. So, a good business model is very forgiving, where you can make a lot of mistakes and still do very well. Whereas a bad business model is very unforgiving. You make a mistake, and it's going to wipe you out."[105]

Michael Hyatt added, "the key is to engineer out of your business surprises—to the best of your ability."

"Cash flow positive" is the technical term that financial analysts use to describe a business that brings in more money than it loses with each sale. In a very simple example, if someone pays you $100 to create a product that costs you $10 to make, and you don't have to spend your $10 until someone pays you $100, you have a cash flow positive business.

Wait a second, you may be thinking, isn't that called profit? But there is a difference between being cash flow positive and profitable, as Meredith Wood, Editor-in-Chief at Fundera, explains,

> "Your cash flow is the money coming in and out of your business on any given day. This working capital is what you use to cover your business expenses, such as payroll, rent, inventory purchases, and so on. Simple, right?
>
> "Your profit, on the other hand, is really only an accounting term that exists on paper. This measurement gives you a basic idea of how much money you have coming in and going out of your business each month, but what it doesn't do is tell you much about your day-to-day operations.
>
> "Keep in mind that many businesses use accrual accounting, which means your revenue and expenses are recorded, regardless of whether or not cash has been exchanged.
>
> "For example, let's say you send out an invoice for $1,000. This $1,000 will be recorded on your profit and loss statement as a profit—even if you don't receive payment for said invoice right away.
>
> "This difference is key when your bills come up as due. If you're still waiting for payment on that invoice, you may not have enough cash on hand to cover the costs, and not having the cash makes you cash flow negative. However, since profit doesn't tell you exactly when money is coming in and going out of your business, you will still appear

profitable on paper, even if that isn't in the bank for you to use."[106]

If you design a business that requires you to spend money creating each product before you get paid by the customer, your business is "cash flow negative." Many (perhaps most) businesses are cash flow negative by design, and so it is possible to succeed this way, but it comes with an extra financial burden, and each sale comes with an extra element of risk.

Becoming cash flow positive is important, because that is the only sustainable way to grow a business while bootstrapping, by paying for production with incoming revenue. Otherwise, each level of business growth will require your investment into production, either in the form of an external investment of cash or a withdrawal from your day-to-day working capital.

Once you are cash flow positive, the sky's the limit on your business growth. Each new sale funds the production of each new product or service, so the only restraint to your business growth is your ability to scale operations with the infrastructure behind what you sell!

Despite the benefits of being cash flow positive, many businesses are cash flow negative by design. For example, many design agencies operate a cash flow negative business, where in a given project they pay their own team of designers and developers thousands of dollars before they send an invoice on to their clients.

Even if everything goes smoothly, and a client pays on time, these businesses are cash flow negative because the cost of delivering the service has already been committed or spent before the income has come in. This keeps the "Accounts Receivable" team employed because there is a high level of built-in risk.

By contrast, if that same agency negotiates a retainer agreement with the same client, where they get paid $10,000 at the first of each month for a set scope of work, then huzzah! They become cash flow positive. So why don't more business owners choose the positive route?

There are many reasons why business owners don't jump straight to a cash flow business structure, but the most obvious one is simply that they don't think about it or aren't aware of the alternative risks. Beyond that, offering customers the option to pay later is also a marketing and sales technique.

The Business Model of the Modern Bank

In the cartoon *Popeye*, the beloved character Wimpy is fond of saying, "I'll gladly pay you Tuesday for a hamburger today!" There are many people who, like Wimpy, will gladly take your product in exchange for an IOU, which is why there is an entire industry category of businesses dedicated to meeting that customer demand. They are called banks.

Banks rely on people taking out loans and paying them back later on to make money because of the interest fees they can earn along the way. Modern banks are built on the idea of "fractional reserve banking" so that even your savings account is really a tool the bank can use to loan more money out to people (the bank is making a gamble that every savings account holder won't try to withdraw their money all at the same time).

While modern banking is complicated, it can be lucrative— but it is also risky, which is why banks tout their FDIC or NCUA insurance, and they expect at least 1% of the loans they make to never be paid back (despite an extensive vetting process).[107] So unless you are actually creating a business using the banking model, don't operate that way. Instead, build a cash flow positive business.

But what if you already have an established business that you just realized is cash flow negative. How do you adapt your business to become cash flow positive over time? I'm glad you asked. Here are four possible solutions:

Solution #1: Charge Up Front

The easiest solution for most businesses to become cash flow positive is to charge up front. By that I mean to adjust your sales process so that customers are paying for your product or service before you pay (in money or time) to deliver it.

Of course, you've probably invested some money into your supplies before a customer walks in the door, but I'll come back to that in a later solution.

In this case, the change may be as simple as sending invoices to clients before a project begins or moving your cash register so that customers pay for their products before your employees create the product in question.

Coffee shops do this especially well, often having you order your coffee and ring it up when you first enter, which requires your payment *and* triggers a printed receipt for the barista to make your coffee at the next station on the line. The truth is, most customers won't blink an eye at paying up front rather than after a product or service is delivered. All you have to do is ask.

I seriously considered acquiring a six-figure lawn care company this year but ultimately didn't. One of the key driving factors in that decision was that they were a cash flow *negative* business, by choice. As a customer myself, I can confirm that they send a monthly invoice (with Net 15 terms) after they've already completed the previous month's work, even though I would happily pay them up front, if they asked.

When I got a chance to review the company's financials, as part of the potential acquisition, I saw that a third of their annual "profit" was stuck in Accounts Receivable, with unpaid invoices from clients stretching back weeks and months! Their accounting software showed that they had made money, but they didn't have cash in the bank, so it wasn't real.

Still, some industries expect to pay later and you may have actually trained your customers to pay for a product or service after it's been delivered. So, what if your customers aren't willing to pay up front? All hope is not lost.

Of course, "get new customers" is always an option, but before you do that, I would encourage you to start by looking for a middle ground where you can ease your customer into a solution that meets their needs while minimizing your cash flow risk.

For service providers (like our design agency example), my favorite solution is the 50/50 invoice, where you request a 50% deposit to begin a project, and the remainder once the project is complete. This puts you and your customer on an even playing field where you each have some skin in the game of the completed project, but your immediate expenses are met.

If you are using Profit First, that 50% deposit may be all you need to cover your operating costs. The key is to make sure you're not overextended so that you've covered your expenses with the deposit if the project should go south along the way and your customer fails to pay the rest of the invoice. At the very least, you can work with some initial payment that minimizes your role as a bank.

If you've genuinely tried your hardest to implement this first solution and your business is still not cash flow positive, consider the next solution (or a combination of multiple solutions).

Solution #2: Incentivize Payment in Full

If, for whatever reason, you are unable to charge your customers full price for a product or service before you invest in the project, this solution is an improvement (whether you're offering a 50/50 invoice or expecting no payments until the project is complete).

The way banks incentivize payment is they charge interest, so the borrower has an incentive to pay promptly and the bank is happy to wait for payment as long as they are paid interest in full.

You are not a bank, and your customers won't expect that, so you should incentivize payment in your own way. Many entrepreneurs have already figured out a creative solution in terms of an early payment or full payment discount.

Many providers do this by offering a 5% or 10% discount for paying an invoice immediately upon receipt, before a project begins. Alternatively, if you typically offer a three-month or six-month payment plan, you might offer a 20% discount on the pricing to "pay in full."

The key is to build the early payment discount into your "regular" price so that if a customer chooses to wait to pay the full balance, you get your own compensation for bank-like services in the form of the pay-in-full discount they didn't take.

This is a double win because you get paid your "interest" but you never called it "interest," so the customer doesn't begrudge you for it. After all, skipping the payment discount was their choice.

Solution #3: Negotiate Your Supply Chain

If there is any inventory, production, or other manufacturing in the process of creating your products or services, you may find it difficult to charge for your products before you've invested in the production process out of your own pocket, your "Cost of Goods Sold."

To some extent, this is to be expected, and many businesses establish a set amount of "Working Capital" to cover the ins and outs of maintaining this inventory supply chain so you don't run out of products to sell.

Working Capital is not an emergency fund, nor is it truly an asset (even though it may appear as such on your Balance Sheet and look like a pile of cash). Working capital is the cost of a cash flow negative business, where you must have money on hand to pay for inventory before you get paid.

So, if this is your case, how can you minimize this need? Increasingly, print-on-demand is a viable option, but there is real power in the economies of scale that come from producing in bulk, so I'm not advocating every product become print-on-demand.

Instead, you should start by negotiating payment with vendors at each step of the production process where you're involved. For example, if you work with a manufacturing company to print custom products you design, or you purchase inventory from wholesale vendors, you should ask them for payment terms.

You would be surprised how many suppliers will agree to 30, 60, or 90-day terms on your invoices. In other words, you can often receive the products you need and have up to three months to pay for them! For your vendor, this may be a decision to become cash flow negative, but to many behind-the-scenes suppliers, that's considered part of doing business.

If you negotiate 60-day terms on supplies, and then you feature those products and sell them (at a markup) within less than 60 days, ta-da! You just became cash flow positive. Of course, you can't guarantee that you will sell the products or services within 60 days, but it's an improvement (this works especially well if you have committed customers who simply haven't paid yet before you order the quantity of product or service time that you need).

When I launched Cowork Columbia as a coworking space with a curated business bookstore, the majority of the books we ordered were directly from Amazon. Sure enough, they offered a commercial card with 90-day payment terms, so we were able to fully stock the bookstore before we opened for business without having to pay cash for that initial stock.

This supply chain solution is tricky because you're still liable to pay an invoice with terms whether you sell your products or not. So, it's not really liability-free inventory, but it does give you extra breathing room to see your cash flow needs coming before they smack you flat on your backside, so at least you can plan ahead!

The sales Cowork Columbia's bookstore made in those first ninety days didn't cover the full cost of an initial inventory order, but they did offset nearly half of the cost, which reduced the burden on business cash flow early on. It may have gone even better if we didn't close the storefront fifty-eight days after opening (because of COVID-19), but even with that, we had time to adapt.

Solution #4: Mind the Gap

If your gears are turning but you are still struggling to find a quick fix to your business model and become cash flow positive, that's okay. The reality is that for some business models, the amount of working capital to remain cash flow positive is prohibitive, but this is not a simple positive/negative switch.

Your goal here is to minimize your cash flow negativity as much as possible, so your final potential solution is to shorten the gap between when you pay to create a product and when you get paid by your customer to the shortest possible window of time.

I worked for Chick-fil-A for years as a Training Director, and they were brilliant at that. They had to be. If they waited to cook food until a customer ordered something, they would need dozens of individual fryers, and each customer would need to wait fifteen minutes for their food.

That may not sound like much, but the average order actually takes less than two minutes, and that is what customers have come to expect. Any longer and the business model starts to fall apart; there simply would not be enough orders to make a profit, given the high cost of equipment, labor, and the facility where the food is made.

Instead, Chick-fil-A (like many similar businesses) estimates the amount of different types of food needed at a given moment based on projections that take into account the previous year's sales combined with the average sales increase (or decrease) in the current month.

They combine this with a "First In, First Out" system where the kitchen crew prepares additional food as they watch popular items run out. At the register, when the team member takes your order, they require payment immediately and then they give you the oldest available food on your tray.

That's right, First In, First Out (or FIFO) means you are actually eating the oldest available chicken sandwich, but because they are constantly monitoring inventory, it still tastes hot and fresh. Chick-fil-A uses a third inventory system based on timers, where they discard food that is past its holding time if it hasn't been sold.

That may sound complicated (or just delicious), but it's served Chick-fil-A and their customers well. They've grown a privately-owned family business to generate $11 billion in annual revenue from 2,470 locations across the United States.[108]

Yes, they still pay for the chicken before you pay for it, but I wouldn't be surprised if they've negotiated payment terms with their primary suppliers. Yes, they still commit to paying their employees to prepare the food before you pay for it, based on their best calculation of demand, and they have payment terms with employees in the form of payroll every two weeks.

When you order your chicken sandwich, waffle fries, and lemonade, they have taken extra steps to become as close as possible to cash flow positive and mind the gap.

How Cash Flow Positive Is Your Business?

Like every other aspect of financial health in your business, being cash flow positive is not simply a yes or no binary decision. There are many ways you can make progress to have as positive a cash flow as possible—and similarly, there are various levels of cash flow positive health.

Depending on the size and scope of your business, and your ability to become cash flow positive, you may want to implement a cash flow tracking system like Michael Hyatt did,

"We've got a Google Sheet that basically uses the conditional formatting so that if the cash balance is negative, that cell goes red, and if it's positive, it goes green. And when it's all green, I sleep well at night. And when there's a red out there in the future, I don't sleep as well. But here's the cool thing about it: I can see it coming. The worst nightmare for a business owner is to suddenly realize on Tuesday afternoon, when you have to communicate your payroll to whoever does your payroll (whether that's an outside service or your CFO) and you realize, 'oh my gosh, we don't have enough cash to cover payroll on Friday.' That is like the worst nightmare you could ever experience. Because then you're scrambling, you're hocking things, you're doing whatever it takes to make that payroll because retaining good people is paramount. What this allows you to do is manage your cash flow to see the bumps in the road and the crises before they happen. So, you can react. If I see a red cell, and it's seven weeks from now, I basically have seven weeks to figure it out. There's no problem my team can't figure out with enough warning, but there's almost no problem we can solve if we're surprised by it."[109]

Increasingly, accounting tools like QuickBooks Online have cash flow forecasting built in, but you may not need those tools if you can design a cash flow positive business. Once you've established working capital, and you're using Profit First to build up your operations account over time, you can watch the sales come in with a confident smile and relax!

So, where is your business right now? Where do you need to grow next? If you haven't already, now is a great time to take the free assessment at YourThriveScore.com to get your business ThriveScore, with a clear framework for how to think about the foundational aspects of financial health in your business.

Claim your **FREE business assessment**
($100 value) and unlock additional resources at
YourThriveScore.com

Conclusion

Serve and Succeed to Survive and Thrive

I wrote this book during, and in response to, the global COVID-19 pandemic—which sparked the Great Lockdown—which then sparked the Great Reset and a massive economic shift across the world.

Still, as you're reviewing the marketing, sales, and finance strategies throughout this book, you may notice that none of them are uniquely useful during an economic crisis. These are principles that can help you build (or rebuild) a profitable business in any economy, truly, whether it's a recession or an economic boom or an average, run-of-the-mill, semi-stable day in the economy of the world.

The world of business has been around for as long as... well, the world!

At its core, business is simply the process of creating:

- Real solutions to
- Real problems for
- Real people.

As soon as mankind started working together, trading goods and services, they discovered certain foundational components of successful business. Over time, the types of goods and services changed considerably, but the foundational rules of business remain true.

Chances are you are already practicing many foundational principles in your business, including some of the strategies taught within this book. On the other hand, you may have very few of these right now, or none at all, and that is okay! Your goal is to add one, and then another, and stay focused on progress—not perfection.

The closest thing you get to a job description as an entrepreneur is that your job is to solve problems for a profit, but that also means your job is to adapt and innovate each day. While the word "pivot" is often used to describe changes in business strategy, Tom Schwab from Interview Valet aptly compared the process more to "tacking,"[110]

"I like the word "tacking." The wind keeps changing, and you're still trying to get to the same spot. But it doesn't mean you go in the same course, and it doesn't mean that every time a sailor changes course a little bit that they made a mistake.

"You gotta come about, you gotta do different things, you've got to get creative. The wind will not blow at the same rate and the same direction. Anybody who thinks that will be disappointed. It's the same way with the business owner. If you think this is going to continue—either the good or the bad forever—you're going to be disappointed and surprised. I love that idea. You know, you can call it tacking with the environment or the wind or even evolving."

At the time, I was admittedly unfamiliar with the concept of tacking, but I was familiar with the idea of success so easy it felt like "sailing." As it turns out, the concept of tacking perfectly describes the journey of an entrepreneur, because a good sailor almost never follows a straight line. Instead, he adjusts his sales in response to the power and direction of the wind, zigging and zagging back and forth to make forward progress (Mike Michalowicz makes a similar connection between tacking and entrepreneurship in *Fix This Next*).

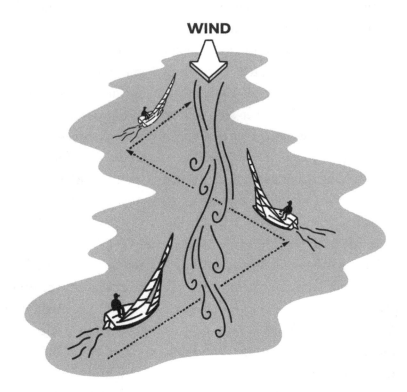

WIND

As you build your business, tacking is a huge part of your day to day work. Sure, you'll have a lot of "the whirlwind"[111] that is required to keep your business operations moving day to day. You'll have invoicing, reconciling, emailing, and general production team meetings—but you'll also have researching, strategizing, and listening to customer stories.

As I'm writing this, in the midst of a 2020 upheaval and economic reset, this is especially clear. As Michael Hyatt put it,

> "If you solve problems at a profit, then you're an entrepreneur. That's what entrepreneurs do. They solve problems at a profit and loss. So, the question I've asked my business coaching clients, particularly business owners, but all entrepreneurs—do people, do your constituents, do your clients have more problems today than they did three months ago? Absolutely. Everybody I know has got more problems. There are all kinds of problems, new problems, problems they've never seen before. More problems than ever before! What that means for an entrepreneur is more opportunity than ever before. So, if you can stay focused on solving your customer's or your client's most vexing problems, you will be successful. It's that simple."[112]

As Michael says, it really is that simple (although solving problems may be complicated, staying focused on problem solving is the simple focus you need). At first glance, that advice seems especially appropriate for the climate as I write this in the year 2020, but as Tom Schwab pointed out in my interview with him, "One thing about the human condition: we're all either in a crisis, coming out of a crisis or going into a crisis. Right?"

Sure enough, Josh Fonger from Work the System was shocked at how true this turned out to be in his experience. As he shared,

"We did a video to get people to buy one of our products seven years ago, and it started off with 'Have you noticed the uncertainty in the market? And have you noticed that global concerns and this and that?' And that video has applied. We replayed that video for years and years and years because the video has always made sense. It's always like 'Yeah, I guess it is kind of uncertain right now. I guess there is a calamity going on right now.' It's always made sense. So, when I watched that video recently, I was like, okay, to think there's going to be a time when there's not a calamity (at least not a calamity the news is gonna report on) is untrue; there always will."[113]

One of the most important takeaways from that insight, that there will always be some kind of uncertainty, crisis, and calamity, is how to respond to each of those. "Look for what I refer to as getting on the right side," advises Jeffrey Shaw, who has been a full-time entrepreneur through three once-in-a-lifetime economic crises. "How can you turn what seems like a dreadful situation into a positive? During the Great Recession, my primary clientele was decimated because they were the wealthy—the ones on the news, right there (some of them were the ones causing the corruption, but that aside)—but I had a whole other group of people who were spending boatloads of money, and I've come to realize that most of them are bankruptcy attorneys. Right? So, they were on the right side of a Great Recession! So, in every case, there's a wrong side or a right side."[114]

As you're building (or rebuilding) your business, you get to decide what to build. You have the sacred responsibility of solving the world's problems (for a profit), and there are real people who are counting on your success. How you build that business is critical.

As Allan Dib aptly describes the importance of business model design: "Some business models are just hell." As he explains,

> "You do the work once, you get paid once, there's no recurring revenue, you've got very high fixed costs, there's very low margins, it's very difficult to satisfy the customer— all of those sorts of things. That's a terrible kind of business. Whereas other business models are awesome! There's recurring revenue, it's easy to get customer satisfaction, the high margins, low overheads, all of those sorts of things. Probably 70% of your success is choosing the right business model; you can be an amazing entrepreneur but just in the wrong business model, and that's going to be the difference between you doing mediocre financially versus you doing very, very well financially. So, a good business model is very forgiving; you can make a lot of mistakes and still do very well. Whereas a bad business model is very unforgiving. You make a mistake, and it's going to wipe you out."[115]

As you're building your business (and regularly assessing your business at YourThriveScore.com), you're going to have to make a lot of difficult choices about which opportunities to chase after, which opportunities to ignore, and which to continue working at when the rewards come slower than you hope (which they usually do). Allan has an extra word of encouragement and advice on this front:

> "How I assess opportunities is asking what's going to really matter in the next four years, five years?" He goes

on to explain, "What's future Allan going to thank me for having done? So, if it's something that's not going to matter in a year or whatever, then it's probably not that great of an opportunity, but if future Allan is really gonna thank me and pat me on the back for having done that, then that's a really good indicator."[116]

So, what is "future you" going to thank you for having done, along with a pat on the back? I can't wait to see it. You've got this. I believe in you. Keep up the good work!

Your friend,
John Meese

Acknowledgments

While it's fun to see my name on the front cover of a book for the first time, it wouldn't be fair for me to take all the credit because writing a book is definitely a full team effort.

First and foremost, I would like to thank my wife, Rachel, for supporting me throughout the entire book-writing process. Thank you for believing in me, loving me, and taking care of our kids during every extra writing session I took to write this book! You inspire me, and there is no way I could have written this book without your care and support. I love you. I owe you.

I would also like to thank Karen Anderson for encouraging me to write the book I was passionate about, rather than the book I thought people wanted from me. You knew, long before a pandemic, that this book was important to every entrepreneur who needed to read it! Thank you for supporting me as a friend, advocate, and publisher.

By extension, I'm grateful for the entire team at Morgan James Publishing; you have been exactly the support team I needed to finish this book. I'd like to thank Bonnie Rauch for leading my author support team to get this book published, Amy Hutto for keeping me on track with the many details behind the scenes, Sissi Haner for taking a passionate attention-to-detail to the editing process with this book, and Emily Mills for brilliantly illustrating key concepts throughout the book itself!

I would not be the entrepreneur I am today without Michael Hyatt, who took a chance on me years ago and placed me front-and-center as a public leader of Platform University and gave me a seat on his leadership team. Thank you, Michael; thank you, Megan; and thank you to everyone at Michael Hyatt & Company for every laugh and lesson along the way.

Thank you to every guest who generously shared your expertise and insight on my podcast (before it even existed). You contributed so much to the stories within this book!

It may be a bit cheesy, but I also have to thank God for the opportunity to co-create something beautiful with this book. Nothing I've written is original; I've simply shared the insights I've learned so far about how this beautiful world works.

Thank You

The world we live in is built by entrepreneurs. The revolutionary technology you and I both use every day, and the seemingly endless supply of resources we have access to, is thanks to hard-working entrepreneurs like you. Thank you.

To succeed as an entrepreneur, you need to become skilled at marketing, finance, and sales—on top of creating products and services that people will pay money for! It's not usually easy, but building a business is good work. Still, it's hard work.

I believe you shouldn't have to figure this out on your own. That's why I wrote this book, but it is also why I serve entrepreneurs every day through the training I publish at JohnMeese.com—I hope you'll stop by to check it out. And if you haven't already, get your free business assessment at YourThriveScore.com!

If there is anything I can do to help you directly, please don't hesitate to contact me by emailing hey@johnmeese.com. Let me know your #1 problem or frustration with your business and how I can help. I look forward to connecting with you soon.

Keep up the good work!

Your friend,
John Meese

About the Author

John Meese is a traditionally trained economist turned serial entrepreneur. He is on a personal mission to eradicate generational poverty by inspiring entrepreneurs and views entrepreneurship as the most effective path to worldwide change.

John is the Dean of Platform University, cofounder of Notable Themes, and Chief Education Officer at Cowork Columbia, an entrepreneur center and coworking space he founded with his wife just fifty-eight days before COVID-19 was confirmed in his community.

Because of COVID-19 exposure followed by a statewide lockdown, John was forced to temporarily close Cowork Columbia's doors, but that became a launchpad for a newly energized focus on helping small business owners adapt their business strategy as they were reeling from the financial, emotional, and health crisis that became the Great Reset.

John lives with his wife and three sons in Columbia, Tennessee, a community affectionately referred to as "Muletown" because of the local heritage as the mule capital of the world.

John has worked closely with multiple clients who have repeatedly hit the Inc. 5000 list of the fastest-growing privately-owned businesses in America, and he currently acts as a strategic advisor for a select group of companies.

John regularly publishes actionable articles, interviews, and videos to share what he learns about building thriving businesses from his own ventures and working directly with clients. You can learn more about John, and connect with him, at JohnMeese.com.

Additional Resources

Did you find this book helpful? Please, share it with a friend who needs it! Simply send them to SurviveAndThriveBook.com. In the meantime, here are some additional resources to help you transform the information within this book into action and results:

- **ThriveScore Assessment:** Fill out a brief questionnaire to get a complimentary business assessment that gives you a numerical ThriveScore based on the strength of your business in terms of finance, marketing, and sales strategy: YourThriveScore.com

- **Survive and Thrive Interviews:** Learn from real-life entrepreneurs as they adapt their own business strategy to a changing economy, including in-depth interviews with guests like Michael Hyatt, Mike Michalowicz, and many more than this book could include: SurviveAndThriveInterviews.com

- **Subscribe to JohnMeese.com:** Most entrepreneurs are overworked and underpaid by the boss in the mirror. On JohnMeese.com, I break down every business success into a repeatable, step-by-step process so you can build a business that fuels your life (rather than the other way around): JohnMeese.com/subscribe

Endnotes

1   Wan, William. "WHO Declares a Pandemic of Coronavirus Disease Covid-19." *The Washington Post*. WP Company, March 11, 2020. https://www.washingtonpost.com/health/2020/03/11/who-declares-pandemic-coronavirus-disease-covid-19/.

2   "Coronavirus Government Response Tracker," Blavatnik School of Government (University of Oxford), accessed August 25, 2020, https://www.bsg.ox.ac.uk/research/research-projects/coronavirus-government-response-tracker.

3   Kochhar, Rakesh. "Unemployment Rose Higher in Three Months of COVID-19 Than It Did in Two Years of the Great Recession." Pew Research Center, July 27, 2020. https://www.pewresearch.org/fact-tank/2020/06/11/unemployment-rose-higher-in-three-months-of-covid-19-than-it-did-in-two-years-of-the-great-recession/.

4   Gopinath, Gita. "The Great Lockdown: Worst Economic Downturn Since the Great Depression." IMF Blog. International Monetary Fund, April 21, 2020. https://blogs.imf.org/2020/04/14/the-great-lockdown-worst-economic-downturn-since-the-great-depression/.

5   Small Business Pulse Survey Data. U.S. Census Bureau. Accessed August 25, 2020. https://portal.census.gov/pulse/data/.

6   Ibid.

7   Ngo, Madeleine. "Thousands of Small Businesses Going Bankrupt in U.S. Are Uncounted in Covid." Bloomberg.com. Bloomberg, August 11, 2020. https://www.bloomberg.com/news/articles/2020-08-11/small-firms-die-quietly-leaving-thousands-of-failures-uncounted.

8   *Avengers: Endgame*. Directed by Joe and Anthony Russo.

United States, Marvel Studios, 2019. Film.

9   *Avengers: Infinity War.* Directed by Joe and Anthony Russo. United States, Marvel Studios, 2018. Film.

10   *Spider-Man: Far From Home.* Directed by John Watts. United States, Marvel Studios and Columbia Pictures, 2019. Film.

11   "September 11 Terror Attacks Fast Facts." CNN. Cable News Network, November 13, 2019. https://www.cnn.com/2013/07/27/us/september-11-anniversary-fast-facts/.

12   Crawford, Neta. "Human Cost Of The Post-9/11 Wars: Lethality And The Need For Transparency." The Watson Institute for International and Public Affairs. Brown University, November 2018. https://watson.brown.edu/costsofwar/files/cow/imce/papers/2018/Human Costs, Nov 8 2018 CoW.pdf.

13   "The USA PATRIOT Act: Preserving Life and Liberty." What is the USA Patriot Web? Dept of Justice. Accessed August 25, 2020. https://www.justice.gov/archive/ll/highlights.htm.

14   Charan, Ram, and Julia Yang. "Jeff Bezos' Philosophy for Amazon Is That It's Always 'Day 1' — Here's What That Means and Why It Works." *Business Insider*, December 10, 2019. https://www.businessinsider.com/jeff-bezos-says-always-day-1-amazon-philosophy-2019-12.

15   Mutikani, Lucia. "What to Know about the Report on America's COVID-Hit GDP." World Economic Forum, July 31, 2020. https://www.weforum.org/agenda/2020/07/covid-19-coronavirus-usa-united-states-econamy-gdp-decline/.

16   *2020 Small Business Profile.* U.S. Small Business Administration Office of Advocacy. Accessed August 25, 2020. https://cdn.advocacy.sba.gov/wp-content/uploads/2020/06/04144224/2020-Small-Business-Economic-Profile-US.pdf.

17   "President Donald J. Trump Remains Committed to Providing Critical Relief for American Small Businesses, Workers, and Healthcare Providers." The White House. The United States Government, April 24, 2020. https://www.whitehouse.gov/briefings-statements/presi-

dent-donald-j-trump-remains-committed-providing-critical-relief-american-small-businesses-workers-healthcare-providers/; Routley, Nick. "The Anatomy of the $2 Trillion COVID-19 Stimulus Bill." *Visual Capitalist*, March 30, 2020. https://www.visualcapitalist.com/the-anatomy-of-the-2-trillion-covid-19-stimulus-bill/.

18   *Merriam-Webster.com Dictionary*, s.v. "entrepreneur," accessed September 10, 2020, https://www.merriam-webster.com/dictionary/entrepreneur.

19   Jens Iversen, Rasmus Jørgensen, and Nikolaj Malchow-Moeller, "Defining and Measuring Entrepreneurship" (June 21, 2010). *Foundations and Trends in Entrepreneurship* Vol. 4, No. 1, pp. 1-63, 2008, Available at SSRN: https://ssrn.com/abstract=1628209

20   Wirtz, Ronald A. "Wanted: Entrepreneurs." Federal Reserve Bank of Minneapolis, June 1, 2008. https://www.minneapolisfed.org/article/2008/wanted-entrepreneurs.

21   Meese, John. "Michael Hyatt." *Survive and Thrive: Interviews with the Best and Brightest Minds in Business Today*. Podcast audio, 2020. https://www.surviveandthriveinterviews.com.

22   Meese, John. "Rabbi Daniel Lapin." *Survive and Thrive: Interviews with the Best and Brightest Minds in Business Today*. Podcast audio, 2020. https://www.surviveandthriveinterviews.com.

23   "Paying Attention: The Attention Economy," *Berkeley Economic Review* (BER Staff, March 31, 2020), https://econreview.berkeley.edu/paying-attention-the-attention-economy.

24   Neri, Antonio. "How the COVID-19 Pandemic Ushered in the Age of Insight." World Economic Forum, July 17, 2020. https://www.weforum.org/agenda/2020/07/how-covid-19-ended-the-information-era-and-ushered-in-the-age-of-insight

25   Ibid.

26   Buchanan, Leigh. "American Entrepreneurship Is Actually Vanishing. Here's Why." Inc.com. *Inc.*, May 2015. https://www.inc.com/magazine/201505/leigh%5C-buchanan/the%5C-vanish-

ing%5C-startups%5C-in%5C-decline.html.

27   Glangchai, Cristal. "Wanted: Entrepreneurs." VentureLab, December 1, 2017. https://venturelab.org/wanted-entrepreneurs.

28   Meese, John. "Tom Schwab." *Survive and Thrive: Interviews with the Best and Brightest Minds in Business Today*. Podcast audio, 2020. https://www.surviveandthriveinterviews.com.

29   Wickman, Gino. *Traction—Get a Grip on Your Business*. Expanded ed. BenBella Books, 2012.

30   Michalowicz, Mike. *Clockwork: Design Your Business to Run Itself*. New York City: Portfolio, 2018.

31   Kelly, Kevin. "1,000 True Fans." *The Technium*. Accessed August 30, 2020. https://kk.org/thetechnium/1000-true-fans/.

32   Ashoka. "Empathy in Business: Indulgence or Invaluable?" *Forbes Magazine*, March 22, 2013. https://www.forbes.com/sites/ashoka/2013/03/22/empathy-in-business-indulgence-or-invaluable/#d-b8705e254e3.

33   Meese, John. "Kevin Whelan." *Survive and Thrive: Interviews with the Best and Brightest Minds in Business Today*. Podcast audio, 2020. https://www.surviveandthriveinterviews.com.

34   Meese, John. "Michael Hyatt." *Survive and Thrive.*

35   Meese, John. "Ray Edwards." *Survive and Thrive: Interviews with the Best and Brightest Minds in Business Today*. Podcast audio, 2020. https://www.surviveandthriveinterviews.com.

36   Maslow, A. H. (1943), "A theory of human motivation," *Psychological Review* 50 no. 4, 370–396. https://doi.org/10.1037/h0054346.

37   Meese, John. "Ray Edwards." *Survive and Thrive.*

38   Edwards, Ray. "The Easiest Way To Sell Anything." *Ray Edwards Show*. February 13, 2013. https://rayedwards.com/048/.

39   Meese, John. "Ray Edwards." *Survive and Thrive.*

40   Pinsker, Joe. "The Psychology Behind Costco's Free Samples." *The Atlantic*. Atlantic Media Company, October 1, 2014. https://www.

theatlantic.com/business/archive/2014/10/the-psychology-behind-cost-cos-free-samples/380969.

41   Meese, John. "Allan Dib." *Survive and Thrive: Interviews with the Best and Brightest Minds in Business Today.* Podcast audio, 2020. https://www.surviveandthriveinterviews.com.

42   Meese, John. "Phillip Stutts." *Survive and Thrive: Interviews with the Best and Brightest Minds in Business Today.* Podcast audio, 2020. https://www.surviveandthriveinterviews.com.

43   "15 Insane Things That Correlate With Each Other." Spurious Correlations. Accessed August 30, 2020. https://www.tylervigen.com/spurious-correlations.

44   "A History of Direct Marketing from 1000BC-1970AD." bakergoodchild, July 19, 2016. https://www.bakergoodchild.co.uk/a-history-of-direct-marketing-up-to-the-1970s/.

45   "Montgomery Ward." *Encyclopedia Britannica.* Encyclopedia Britannica, Inc., February 13, 2020. https://www.britannica.com/biography/Montgomery-Ward.

46   "How Much Coca-Cola Spends on Advertising." Investopedia, May 18, 2020. https://www.investopedia.com/articles/markets/081315/look-cocacolas-advertising-expenses.asp.

47   Guttmann, A. "Walt Disney: Ad Spend 2019." Statista, March 11, 2020. https://www.statista.com/statistics/685554/walt-disney-ad-expense.

48   Meese, John. "Brian Kurtz." *Survive and Thrive: Interviews with the Best and Brightest Minds in Business Today.* Podcast audio, 2020. https://www.surviveandthriveinterviews.com.

49   *The Power Parthenon Strategy of Geometric Business Growth.* (Rolling Hills Estates: The Abraham Group, Inc.), https://s3-us-west-2.amazonaws.com/jayabrahamassets/Wiki+Resouces/The%2B-Power%2BParthenon%2B8-19-05+(1).pdf.

50   Meese, John. "Ray Edwards." *Survive and Thrive.*

51   *The Power Parthenon Strategy of Geometric Business*

Growth. (Rolling Hills Estates: The Abraham Group, Inc.), https://s3-us-west-2.amazonaws.com/jayabrahamassets/Wiki+Resouces/The%2B-Power%2BParthenon%2B8-19-05+(1).pdf.

52   Meese, John. "Ray Edwards." *Survive and Thrive.*

53   Barry, Nathan. "Why Email Subscribers Are Better than Social Media Followers." ConvertKit, November 18, 2019. https://convertkit.com/email-subscriber-worth.

54   Meese, John. "Should You Delete Every Social Media Profile You Have?" John Meese, October 31, 2019. https://johnmeese.com/social-media/.

55   Meese, John. "Brian Kurtz." *Survive and Thrive.*

56   Liu, Richard. "5 Growth Strategy Case Studies and Key Takeaways." Medium. Yought Blog-Marketing and Tech, July 5, 2019. https://medium.com/yought-blog/5-growth-strategy-case-studies-and-key-takeaways-27e208e84a97.

57   Wicked Reports. "Is My Marketing Doing Anything?" Archived PowerPoint presentation. https://f.hubspotusercontent30.net/hubfs/5995083/PDF%20for%20download/Benchmark%20Report%20Lead%20Magnet.pptx

58   Meese, John. "Casey Graham." *Survive and Thrive: Interviews with the Best and Brightest Minds in Business Today.* Podcast audio, 2020. https://www.surviveandthriveinterviews.com.

59   Sheridan, Marcus. *They Ask, You Answer: A Revolutionary Approach to Inbound Sales, Content Marketing, and Today's Digital Consumer.* Hoboken, NJ: John Wiley & Sons, 2019.

60   Bhandari, Madhav. "How ConvertKit Brings in ~$6 Million Annually through Their Affiliates." Remote Marketing, November 25, 2019. https://remotemarketing.org/convertkit-affiliate.

61   "Check out ConvertKit on Inc.com!" Inc.com, August 11, 2020. https://www.inc.com/profile/convertkit.

62   ConvertKit's Revenue Dashboard on Baremetrics. Accessed August 30, 2020. https://convertkit.baremetrics.com/.

63   "Habit 4: Think Win-Win." Franklin Covey. Accessed August 30, 2020. https://www.franklincovey.com/the-7-habits/habit-4.html.
64   Gillath, Omri and Angela J. Bahns and Fiona Ge and Christian S. Crandall, "Shoes as a source of first impressions," *Journal of Research in Personality* 46, no. 4. http://dx.doi.org/10.1016/j.jrp.2012.04.003.
65   "Apple Revenue Breakdown by Product." Statista Research Department. Statista, August 7, 2020. https://www.statista.com/statistics/382260/segments-share-revenue-of-apple/.
66   Warrillow, John. *The Automatic Customer: Creating a Subscription Business in Any Industry*. London: Portfolio Penguin, 2016.
67   Meese, John. "Mike McDerment." *Survive and Thrive: Interviews with the Best and Brightest Minds in Business Today*. Podcast audio, 2020. https://www.surviveandthriveinterviews.com.
68   Meese, John. "Allan Dib." *Survive and Thrive*.
69   Akins, Anna. "Five Things You Need to Know about Chick-Fil-A Waffle Fries." *The Chicken Wire*. Chick-fil-A, June 28, 2019. https://thechickenwire.chick-fil-a.com/inside-chick-fil-a/five-things-you-need-to-know-about-chick-fil-a-waffle-fries.
70   Meese, John. "Scott Beebe." *Survive and Thrive: Interviews with the Best and Brightest Minds in Business Today*. Podcast audio, 2020. https://www.surviveandthriveinterviews.com.
71   *The ROI from Marketing to Existing Online Customers*. Adobe Digital Index. Accessed August 25, 2020. http://success.adobe.com/assets/en/downloads/whitepaper/13926.digital_index_loyal_shoppers_report.pdf.
72   *Merriam-Webster.com Dictionary*, s.v. "remarkable," accessed August 30, 2020, https://www.merriam-webster.com/dictionary/remarkable.
73   Reiley, Laura. "The Sky Is Falling for Fast Food, but Not for Chick-Fil-A. Here's Why." *The Washington Post*. WP Company, June 19, 2019. https://www.washingtonpost.com/business/2019/06/19/

chick-fil-a-becomes-third-largest-restaurant-chain-us/.

74   Cathy, Dan T., "Going the Second Mile," Dec 15, 2010, You-Tube video, 6:35, https://www.youtube.com/watch?v=i8DGOcxXA34.

75   Meese, John. "Caleb Mathis." *Survive and Thrive: Interviews with the Best and Brightest Minds in Business Today*. Podcast audio, 2020. https://www.surviveandthriveinterviews.com.

76   Michalowicz, Mike. *Fix This Next: Make the Vital Change That Will Level Up Your Business*. New York: Portfolio/Penguin, 2020.

77   Kelly, Kevin. "1,000 True Fans." *The Technium*.

78   Marshall, Perry S. *80/20 Sales and Marketing: The Definitive Guide to Working Less and Making More*. Irvine, CA: Entrepreneur Press, 2013.

79   Meese, John. "Pat Flynn." *Survive and Thrive: Interviews with the Best and Brightest Minds in Business Today*. Podcast audio, 2020. https://www.surviveandthriveinterviews.com.

80   Meese, John. "Sean Harper." *Survive and Thrive: Interviews with the Best and Brightest Minds in Business Today*. Podcast audio, 2020. https://www.surviveandthriveinterviews.com.

81   Meese, John. "Pat Flynn." *Survive and Thrive*.

82   "The Four Rules: Age Your Money." YNAB: You Need A Budget. Accessed August 30, 2020. https://www.youneedabudget.com/the-four-rules/#rule-four.

83   Meese, John. "Josh Fonger." *Survive and Thrive: Interviews with the Best and Brightest Minds in Business Today*. Podcast audio, 2020. https://www.surviveandthriveinterviews.com.

84   "Small Business Pulse Survey." Small Business Pulse Survey Data. U.S. Census. Accessed August 30, 2020. https://portal.census.gov/pulse/data/.

85   Hudson, Erin. "Retailers exposed: Who's paying rent and who's not." The Real Deal New York, April 22, 2020. https://therealdeal.com/2020/04/22/retailers-exposed-whos-paying-rent-and-whos-

not/.

86   Timestaff. "Swimming Naked When the Tide Goes Out." *Money*. Money, April 2, 2009. https://money.com/swimming-naked-when-the-tide-goes-out/.

87   Lidow, Derek. "Why Two-Thirds of the Fastest-Growing Companies Fail." *Fortune*. Fortune, March 7, 2016. https://fortune.com/2016/03/07/fast-growth-companies-fail/.

88   Meese, John. "Josh Fonger." *Survive and Thrive*.

89   Locke, Edwin A., and Gary P. Latham. "Building a Practically Useful Theory of Goal Setting and Task Motivation: A 35-Year Odyssey." *American Psychologist*57, no. 9, September 2002. https://www-2.rotman.utoronto.ca/facbios/file/09 - Locke & Latham 2002 AP.pdf.

90   Hyatt, Michael. *Your Best Year Ever: A 5-Step Plan for Achieving Your Most Important Goals*. Grand Rapids, MI: Baker Books, a division of Baker Publishing Group, 2019.

91   "The Best Goal-Achievement Strategy." The Raymond Aaron Group. Accessed August 30, 2020. http://aaron.com/2013/08/13/the-best-goal-achievement-strategy/.

92   Meese, John. "Raymond Aaron." *Survive and Thrive: Interviews with the Best and Brightest Minds in Business Today*. Podcast audio, 2020. https://www.surviveandthriveinterviews.com.

93   Ibid.

94   "The Best Goal-Achievement Strategy." http://aaron.com/2013/08/13/the-best-goal-achievement-strategy/.

95   Otar, Chad. "Council Post: What Percentage Of Small Businesses Fail—And How Can You Avoid Being One Of Them?" *Forbes Magazine*, August 21, 2019. https://www.forbes.com/sites/forbes-financecouncil/2018/10/25/what-percentage-of-small-businesses-fail-and-how-can-you-avoid-being-one-of-them/.

96   Michalowicz, Mike. *Profit First: Transform Your Business from a Cash-Eating Monster to a Money-Making Machine*. New York: Portfolio, 2017.

97   "Parkinson's Law." *The Economist Newspaper*. Accessed August 30, 2020. https://www.economist.com/news/1955/11/19/parkinsons-law.

98   Meese, John. "Mike Michalowicz." *Survive and Thrive: Interviews with the Best and Brightest Minds in Business Today*. Podcast audio, 2020. https://www.surviveandthriveinterviews.com.

99   Michalowicz, Mike. *Profit First: Transform Your Business from a Cash-Eating Monster to a Money-Making Machine*. New York: Portfolio, 2017.

100   Meese, John. "Scott Beebe." *Survive and Thrive*.

101   Meese, John. "Mike Michalowicz." *Survive and Thrive*.

102   Benzinga, Dave Royse. "This Day In Market History: Lehman Brothers Collapses." Yahoo! Finance. Yahoo!, September 16, 2019. https://finance.yahoo.com/news/day-market-history-lehman-brothers-192808024.html.

103   Meese, John. "Michael Hyatt." *Survive and Thrive*.

104   Ibid.

105   Meese, John. "Allan Dib." *Survive and Thrive*.

106   Wood, Meredith. "Cash Flow-Positive vs. Profitability: What's the Difference?" Fundbox Blog, September 28, 2018. https://fundbox.com/blog/cash-flow-positive-vs-profitability-whats-difference/.

107   "Delinquency Rate on Commercial and Industrial Loans, All Commercial Banks." FRED, August 25, 2020. https://fred.stlouisfed.org/series/DRBLACBS.

108   Taylor, Kate. "Chick-Fil-A Is the Third-Largest Fast-Food Chain in America, and That Should Terrify Wendy's and Burger King." *Business Insider*. Insider Inc., May 14, 2020. https://www.businessinsider.com/chick-fil-a-third-largest-fast-food-chain-us-sales-2020-5.

109   Meese, John. "Michael Hyatt." *Survive and Thrive*.

110   Meese, John. "Tom Schwab." *Survive and Thrive*.

111   McChesney, Chris, Sean Covey, and Jim Huling. *The 4 Disciplines of Execution: Achieving Your Wildly Important Goals*. New

York: Free Press, 2016.

112   Meese, John. "Michael Hyatt." *Survive and Thrive.*

113   Meese, John. "Josh Fonger." *Survive and Thrive.*

114   Meese, John. "Jeffrey Shaw." *Survive and Thrive: Interviews with the Best and Brightest Minds in Business Today.* Podcast audio, 2020. https://www.surviveandthriveinterviews.com.

115   Meese, John. "Allan Dib." *Survive and Thrive.*

116   Ibid.

A free ebook edition is available with the purchase of this book.

To claim your free ebook edition:

1. Visit MorganJamesBOGO.com
2. Sign your name CLEARLY in the space
3. Complete the form and submit a photo of the entire copyright page
4. You or your friend can download the ebook to your preferred device

Morgan James
BOGO™

A **FREE** ebook edition is available for you or a friend with the purchase of this print book.

CLEARLY SIGN YOUR NAME ABOVE

Instructions to claim your free ebook edition:
1. Visit MorganJamesBOGO.com
2. Sign your name CLEARLY in the space above
3. Complete the form and submit a photo of this entire page
4. You or your friend can download the ebook to your preferred device

Print & Digital Together Forever.

Snap a photo

Free ebook

Read anywhere